Population and labour

Corrigendum

Please substitute the figure reproduced below
for figure 16 on page 137.

Figure 16.   The dependency load (based on 1970 population)

| | Population under 15 years of age | for every 100 persons aged 15 to 64 |
| | Population aged 65 and over | |

Source: based on United Nations Population Division statistics.

Corrigendum

Population and labour

A popular account of the implications
of rapid population growth for
the training, employment and welfare
of workers

Published with the financial support of the
United Nations Fund for Population Activities

International Labour Office   Geneva

ISBN 92-2-101024-4

First published 1973

PRINTED BY IMPRIMERIES POPULAIRES, GENEVA (SWITZERLAND)

FOREWORD

This survey attempts to answer certain specific questions about rapid population growth and labour problems. Why the world's population is expanding as it is and what, if anything, should be done about it are questions that lie strictly outside the scope of the survey. It was felt, however, that it might be helpful for the non-specialist reader if the book were to open with a sketch of the general background, and this is presented in the first four chapters. This introductory section must not be taken as an attempt to paint a complete picture: that has been done with much greater thoroughness in a number of publications, including several issued by the United Nations. Nor should the survey as a whole be looked upon as anything other than a rapid reconnaissance of the field, drawing upon whatever information is currently available. It is, in effect, a summary of the literature on the subject such as existed in 1973. It is not based on the ILO research into certain aspects of the population question (including the effect of demographic factors on employment and the relationship between social security and family size) which is now under way as a part of the World Employment Programme. It will be some time, however, before this research is completed, and in the meantime it is hoped that the present survey will at least clarify the issues and throw into relief the gravity of the problem.

In presenting the general reader with a broad review of the influences and consequences of rapid population growth, the author has included both well established scientific facts and controversial matters on which there are conflicting opinions. It is not always possible to present the many opposing views or to draw conclusions of permanent value on subjects where systematic research is still in its infancy. It should be emphasised, therefore, that the ILO realises that there are divergent opinions concerning population questions. The ILO is also well aware that any discussion of family planning raises moral, ethical and religious issues and controversial interpretations of social and economic data on which it is difficult to reflect the views of all concerned, and the views expressed in this book are in no way to be considered as dogmatic or as necessarily representing the views of the ILO.

As the author points out, population limitation is no panacea. Rapid population growth is not the sole cause of the difficulties faced by developing countries, and family planning alone is not a sufficient programme for developing the economies and the cultures of the Third World; for no decrease in the birth rate can release the developing countries from the need energetically to press for radical agrarian reforms, the modernisation of agricultural production, industrialisation, higher educational and cultural standards, and a generally improved standard of living.

The reader should be warned that the expressions "developing countries", "Third World", "less developed regions", and so on, used as synonyms in the text, may not always refer to exactly the same geographical areas. That is because different authorities, even within the United Nations system, have their own definitions of what constitutes a "developing" country. These differences are marginal, however, and do not interfere with the conclusions. It should also be noted that, for the sake of simplicity, the effects of international migration of labour have not been discussed in these pages. Migration, obviously, is itself partly a consequence of population pressure; it will aggravate the difficulties in some countries and ease them in others, but it cannot significantly alter the general picture. *Internal* migration, from the rural areas to the towns, is another matter.

This survey was undertaken at the request of the 51st Session of the International Labour Conference, and has been prepared with the financial support of the United Nations Fund for Population Activities. It has been written by Robert Plant, a British national born in East Africa, who later served as a lecturer on economic and social problems at the Kampala Labour College, Uganda. He takes a deep and personal interest in Africa's development.

CONTENTS

THE BACKGROUND

THE PROBLEMS

Acknowledgments

The International Labour Office wishes to make acknowledgment to the following for permission to reproduce photographs in this book: Bibliothèque publique et universitaire, Geneva (facing p. 6, *a*); World Health Organization, Geneva (facing pp. 6, *b*; 119, *b*; 134); Centre international de reportages et d'information culturelle (CIRIC), Geneva (facing pp. 7; 70; 71, *b*; 86; 87, *a*); Camera Press Ltd., London/Len Sirman Press, Geneva (facing p. 71, *a*); Len Sirman Press, Geneva (facing p. 118). The remaining photographs are taken from the ILO Photo Library, Geneva.

Acknowledgment is also extended to the Parents' Magazine Press, New York, in respect of figure 1 on p. 5.

THE BACKGROUND

LIVING AND DYING

1

Kipchoge Keino, the 1968 Olympic 1500 metres champion, was born in Kenya's Nandi Hills in 1940. He was the sixth child, of whom four had died at birth. Four years later when his mother, still a young woman, was bearing her seventh child, both she and the baby died. Tragedies like this are happily much rarer today, one generation later, and they are becoming still rarer with every year that passes, as newly introduced social improvements begin to take effect. One of the consequences is that the population of Kenya is doubling every 21 years.

It is, however, not so much the high birth rates that account for the so-called "population explosion" in the developing countries; it is rather the continuing fall in death rates, and as this fall is by no means over (for instance, even today in India two-thirds of all deaths of women aged between 15 and 45 are related to child-bearing), we may expect populations to go on expanding for a long time to come.

Nevertheless, the population explosion must come to an end some day, unless human beings are going to live for ever. Provided that disaster does not intervene, the death rate will presumably fall eventually to much the same level all over the world, and the population growth curve will then flatten out. At present, death rates in the developing countries are still approximately double those in the more developed countries (see Annex I).

Another way of putting this would be to say that man's life span should some day be nearly equal the world over and that, when this point is reached, population growth will have fallen everywhere to the relatively low rate now recorded in the world's healthiest societies, other things—including birth rates—being equal. Today, a person born in the poorest regions of the world can expect to live for barely 40 years, whilst the figure for the wealthiest regions is approaching 75 years. The whole of Europe, North America, Australia, New Zealand, Japan and the USSR have passed the 70 mark. At the other extreme,

3

the average life span is only slightly over 40 years in equatorial Africa; 50 years in northern Africa, southern Africa and Asia; and 60 years in Latin America. There is still a long way to go.

Health experts say that 75 years is likely to remain the limit to the average life span, unless there is a revolutionary breakthrough enabling man to control the ageing process. With that important proviso, then, there seems to be a biological barrier beyond which the human life span is unlikely to be pushed by the conquest of disease. At present, the expectation of life is rising in most parts of the Third World: for example, largely as a result of the reduction of disease, the average man's life span in Mexico lengthened from 36 to nearly 60 years between 1934 and 1964. In Mauritius it rose from 38 to 58 in the two decades ending in 1960. Expectation of life in India was 27 years in the 1920s, rose to 32 by 1945 and is now about 50 for those who survive the first year.

The conquest of a single killer disease can have a wonderful effect on man's chances of living longer. For instance, in Sri Lanka the first major malaria campaign in 1946-47 saw a drop in the crude death rate from 20 per 1,000 of the population to 14 per 1,000 in a single year, and this was no flash in the pan. Average mortality during the 15 years following the campaign settled at 12 per 1,000 of the population: during the previous 15 years it had been 22 per 1,000.

As the major killer diseases come under control, it may be that general living standards will play a relatively bigger part in prolonging human life. The question does not concern us at the moment. The point is that it is falling mortality levels, however achieved, rather than surging birth rates that account for most of the rapid population expansion now taking place in the Third World. This does not mean that populations are growing older—quite the reverse. The lives that are being saved are those of children and young people.

THE TWO WORLDS

Where reliable figures are available, they show that birth rates have not changed significantly in the developing countries over recent years. They also show, however, that birth rates are very much higher in such countries than in more sophisticated societies, being indeed on average more than twice as high (see Annex I and figure 1). The difference is so marked that Goran Ohlin observed as recently as 1967 that fertility seemed to provide a sharper criterion for distinguishing underdeveloped countries from developed ones than any other social or economic variable. Yet birth rates in Europe were very much higher at the beginning of the century than they are today. They have fallen unobtrusively to their present levels without any public exhortation or encouragement. The question demographers ask themselves is: will a time arrive when a similar decline will begin to occur spontaneously in the countries of the Third

Figure 1.   Average number of children born per woman, at age 44

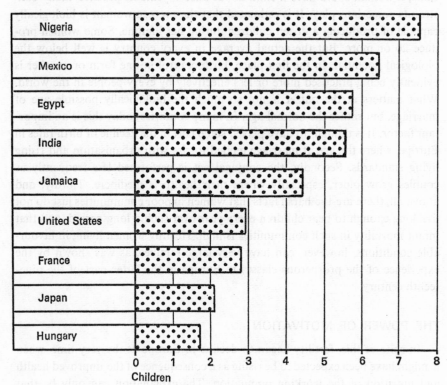

Source: Todd Fisher, *Our overcrowded world* (New York, Parents' Magazine Press, 1969), p. 230.

World? If so, when will that point be reached, and how rapidly will the decline take effect?

For statesmen concerned with population problems the corresponding questions are: can such a reversal come in time to alleviate the social stresses of rapid population growth? If not, can the change be hastened by public policy? Not all governments accept that there is a serious problem, but those that do so are obliged to address themselves to the possibility of curbing fertility, because it would be unthinkable to redress the balance by manipulating mortality rates. On the contrary, they are very properly doing their utmost to lengthen their peoples' expectation of life, thereby cancelling out, as it were, the results achieved at one end of the life span by progress made at the other. This is the built-in paradox of population policy. It accounts for the fact that all experts foretell rapid growth of the world's population for many years to come.

In principle, a normal woman can bear children from the age of 15 to 45. Childbirth is followed by a short sterile period, so that, under favourable conditions, a woman could have a child about once a year. In practice many constraints come into play. It is estimated that the average woman is biologically capable of producing a dozen children during her lifetime. Some women produce 20 or more. But the actual average in every country is well below the biological potential. In the first place, birth control in one form or another is evidently being practised more or less effectively by every people in the world. What matters at the outset is not so much the biologically possible age of marriage, but rather the normal age. In many countries today this is an important factor. It is thought to have played some part in the decline of birth rates in Europe, where the age at marriage tended to rise with urbanisation and rising living standards. Secondly, the conjugal act is performed less frequently as couples grow older, especially where their health is mediocre. Thirdly, and above all, there are the harsh facts that women in poor communities just do not live long enough to bear children every year over such a long period, and that infant mortality in such communities is high. Healthy women living in favourable conditions, however, can have very large families, as was shown by the experience of the prosperous classes in Europe in the latter part of the nineteenth century.

THE POWER OF MOTIVATION

In spite of this, fertility began to decline in Europe at the very time when it might have been expected to be rising as a consequence of the improved health and nutrition of the working population. The explanation can only be that married couples privately decided to limit their families, notwithstanding the fact that contraception was, if anything, condemned at that time by the moral code. All the evidence, in fact, indicates that in all societies, at all times, couples who have ceased to desire more children take steps to avoid having them. It is motivation, not contraceptive technology, that is decisive.

Recent surveys in a number of developing countries have revealed that motivation in these countries is already fairly widespread, if not yet strong enough to make a permanent impact. The results have naturally varied in detail, but the general picture is remarkably consistent. About three-quarters of the population (ranging from 65 to 80 per cent) approved of family planning, about three-fifths (50-70 per cent) would like to know more about contraceptive methods, and about half of the couples with three or more children (40-60 per cent) would prefer to have no more. At the same time, only about one-tenth (5-20 per cent) as yet actually practised any form of family limitation.[1] These

---

[1] The results of these surveys are summarised in United Nations: *Human fertility and national development: a challenge to science and technology* (New York, 1971; Sales No.: E.71.II.A.12).

AT HOME IN SWITZERLAND, 1880 (*Above*)
AT SCHOOL IN GHANA, 1973 (*Below*)

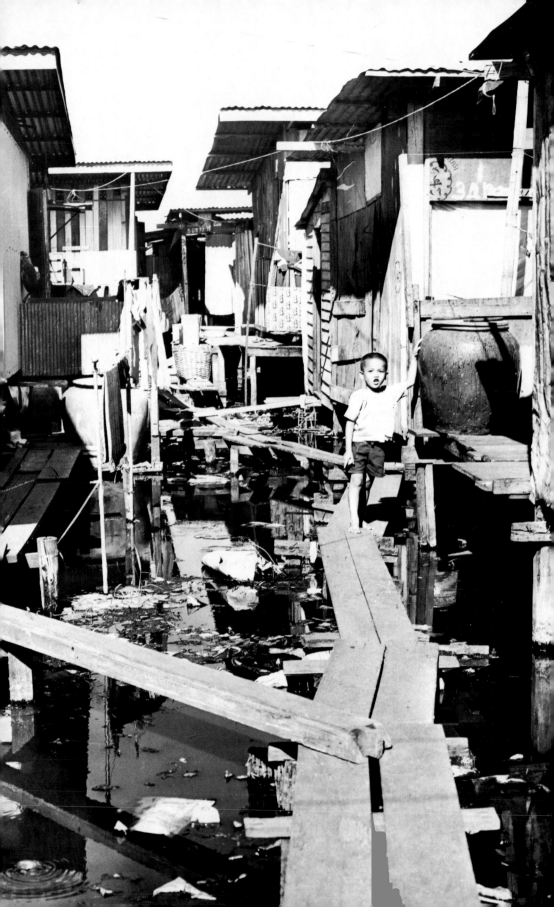

figures suggest that the long-awaited retreat from the cradle may begin sooner in certain parts of the developing world than was previously thought likely, especially in countries where every assistance is given to couples who wish to limit their families.[1]

Speculation about the underlying reasons why European couples began limiting their families more than half a century ago is not very helpful in any analysis of the motives of present-day couples in the developing countries. Such an analysis would have to be based on research in the developing countries today, with their very different cultures and social pressures and against a completely different world background. The fertility decline has already begun in a few limited areas in the Far East and in the Caribbean, and tentative forecasts have been made as to when it is likely to start in a number of other developing countries. In Europe the records suggest a close relationship between educational standards and the fall in fertility, and a similar connection appears to be supported by the comparative statistics of a number of developing countries; but it does not follow that demographic change can be accelerated just by teaching more people to read and write. The literacy level may be no more than a reflection of wider and deeper social changes, which cause young people to see the world through different eyes.

THE PROSPECT

In the year 1750 the world's population was in the region of 790 million people. At the beginning of the present century the human stock numbered about 1,650 million. Today the figure is well over 3,600 million. Where will it stand when the century ends, less than 30 years from now? If present trends were to continue, estimates show that the total would exceed 7,800 million. This estimate takes into account the probable changes in mortality rates, as the expectation of life in different regions moves steadily towards its limit; but what it does *not* reflect is any possible decline in fertility.

That, indeed, is the great unknown. Present birth rates in developing countries average about 40 per 1,000. The latest United Nations projections (made available to the author but not yet published at the time of writing) contain forecasts based on four different assumptions: (1) no significant change in fertility (giving the 7,800 million estimate cited above); (2) a relatively quick onset of lower fertility rates; (3) a relatively slow onset of these rates; and (4) a medium variant, considered to be the most likely, which assumes that birth rates in the developing countries will fall to an average of about 34 per 1,000

---

[1] In Japan the crude birth rate was halved in 10 years, falling from 34 per 1,000 in 1947 to 17 in 1957. A drop of this order is exceptional, but it seems to indicate that a decline in fertility sets in rapidly when economic development passes a certain point.

Population and labour

Table 1.   World population prospects as assessed in 1968 (millions)

Area	1970	Constant fertility		High variant		Medium variant		Low variant	
		1985	2000	1985	2000	1985	2000	1985	2000
More developed areas	1 090	[1]	1 477	[1]	1 467	1 275	1 454	[1]	1 438
Less developed areas	2 542	3 925	6 369	3 876	5 650	3 658	5 061	3 473	4 523
Southern Asia	1 126	1 778	2 989	1 763	2 617	1 693	2 354	1 614	2 119
Eastern Asia[2]	930	1 341	1 963	1 296	1 627	1 182	1 424	1 106	1 274
Africa	344	531	873	549	906	530	818	512	734
Latin America and Caribbean	283	457	760	450	713	435	652	421	600
World	*3 632*	*5 202*	*7 846*	*5 153*	*7 118*	*4 933*	*6 515*	*4 747*	*5 962*

[1] Up to 1985, only one variant was prepared for more developed regions; the projections for these regions up to 2000 have 1985 as a basis.   [2] Including Japan, a developed country.
Source: United Nations Population Division.

by the year 1985 and then continue declining to the end of the century. These lead to a low estimate of the world's population at the century's end of 6,000 million, a high estimate of 7,000 million and a medium estimate of 6,500 million. Thus, even allowing for a steady decline in fertility, the time-lag between the higher and lower estimates of when it might take effect makes a difference to the probable world population less than 30 years from now of no fewer than 1,000 million (table 1 and figures 2 and 3).

The figure of 6,500 million put forward under the medium fertility assumption therefore represents a total world population that is four times bigger than at the beginning of the century and nearly twice as big as in 1970. Moreover, of that increase of close on 3,000 million human beings to feed, clothe, house, educate and care for in the next 30 years, it is estimated that 2,500 million will be in the less developed areas.

To obtain a glimpse of possible trends beyond the year 2000, we have to turn back to earlier projections, bearing in mind that these are probably underestimates. The world's population by the year 2050 would be about 30,000 million if present birth rates continued. On the United Nations low fertility assumption it would be at least 11,000 million, and on the medium fertility assumption it would be at least 15,000 million—that is, over four times our present population.

It should be emphasised that these are theoretical calculations, on assumptions which become more uncertain the farther one tries to penetrate into the future. If we assume that the world's population will continue increasing in number, however slowly, we can obviously reach any total we like by carrying the projection far enough. A point can be reached, therefore, when the exercise

Figure 2.   World population, 1750–2000

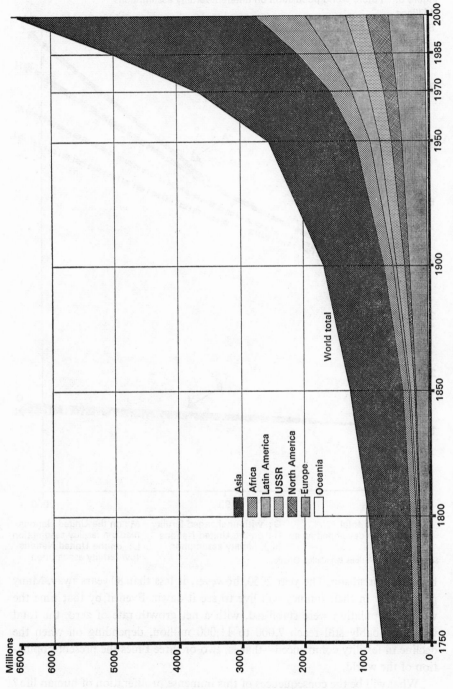

Source: estimates 1750–1950 from United Nations: *Human fertility and national development : a challenge to science and technology*, op. cit.; estimates from 1970 based on United Nations medium fertility assumption.

Figure 3.   Future world population on different fertility assumptions

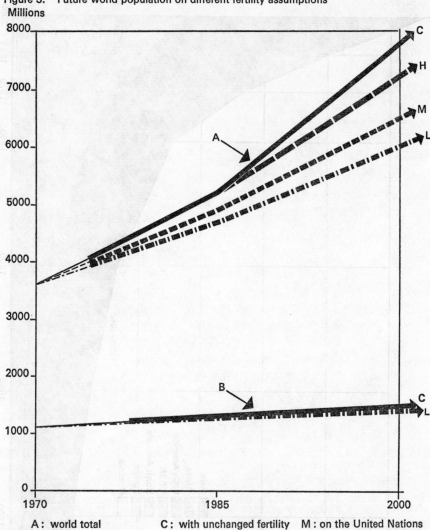

Millions

A : world total   C : with unchanged fertility   M : on the United Nations
B : more developed areas H : on the United Nations   medium fertility assumption
                          high fertility assumption   L : on the United Nations
Source : United Nations Population Division.   low fertility assumption

becomes unrealistic. The year 2050, however, is less than 80 years away. Many people now in their infancy will live to see it dawn. Even if by that time the world's population were stabilised, with a net growth rate of zero, the total would probably still reach 7,000 to 11,000 million, depending on when the decline in fertility commenced—that is, two or three times the present population of the world.

What will be the consequences of this immense proliferation of human life?

A RACE AGAINST TIME

2

The first question that naturally springs to mind is: just how many people can our world support? Twenty years ago the United Nations Population Division, in a study entitled *The determinants and consequences of population trends*, quoted a number of expert calculations of the carrying capacity of the earth. These were based on estimates of what was thought to be the maximum feasible level of world food production, divided by the quantity of food needed to sustain a human life. The most optimistic figure was that of the scientist Penck, published in 1941, who put the total at a maximum of 16,000 million. The most pessimistic was that of Pearson and Harper, which appeared in 1945. They estimated the maximum at 2,800 million persons living at Asian standards of nutrition, or 2,100 million with European standards. Today the world is supporting approximately 3,700 million people at different levels. The maximum Pearson and Harper believed the earth could carry at a poor level of subsistence was passed about 1954.

These prognostications are quoted not to ridicule their authors but simply to show that nobody really knows the answer. Some more recent estimates are more cheerful. In 1956 Harrison Brown put the carrying capacity of the earth at 50,000 million people, and the Russian scientist Malin has claimed that with a great enough effort 9,330 million hectares of the earth's surface could be brought under the plough. Not counting Antarctica, the land surface of the earth is about 13,600 million hectares, of which some 1,450 million are cultivated at present, with a further 2,580 million in use as meadow and pasture. Desert and other barren lands cover 5,420 million hectares. If the area of farmland were raised to the 9,330 million hectares Malin believes possible, he estimates that the earth could support from 65,000 million to 130,000 million people; and if man discovered how to convert solar energy into food the feedable world population would begin to approach 1 million million, or nearly 300 times the present total.

A generation that has seen men ride on the moon would hesitate to discount such forecasts, although common sense suggests that it would be imprudent to base present-day policies on these high expectations. In the present state of scientific knowledge, expert opinion cautiously puts the ultimate carrying capacity of the earth at about 15,000 million persons. Whatever the correct figure may be, then, it seems that the earth could in fact sustain several times its present population. The question is not, at the moment, whether the resources are there, but whether they can be harnessed fast enough to provide employment and a satisfactory standard of living for the swelling multitude. It is a race against time.

So far, the race has been a close-run contest. In the 25 or 30 years following the Second World War, food production has in fact just about managed to keep up with population growth. When one considers that the world's population grew by approximately 50 per cent during that period, this is no mean achievement. In the less developed regions of the world the pace was even faster, with populations growing by nearly two-thirds between 1945 and 1970. The average person had, if anything, a little more to eat at the end of the period than at the beginning. But a little more, alas, is not enough. Many millions of the world's people are already badly fed, and millions more are underfed. The Food and Agriculture Organization estimates that six out of every ten people in the developing countries suffer from malnutrition. It has stated that food intake per person in these countries, containing more than 70 per cent of the world's people, ought to be raised by more than 50 per cent by the end of the century if an adequate diet is to be provided. With populations growing as they are in the Third World, that would entail a total expansion of food supplies in these regions exceeding 200 per cent. The question posed above in a general way can thus be expressed more precisely: can the developing countries treble their food output in 30 years?

The same question may be asked about fuel and raw materials. Even if untapped resources exist in the required quantitites, can fresh deposits be discovered and exploited fast enough? Or, if we are to rely on synthetic substitutes, can scientists develop them fast enough? Can houses be built fast enough? Schools? Hospitals? Factories? Electricity generating stations? Roads and railways? And can doctors be trained fast enough—not to mention teachers, administrators, technicians and skilled workers?

A DOUBLE DRAIN

It is obvious that a society with a very high reproduction rate will have to expand school, medical and other social facilities for young people much more rapidly than a society with a low reproduction rate, if it hopes to maintain or improve social standards. This must be true whatever a country's economic strength. It is also true that this "demographic investment" will consume resources which might otherwise become available for economic development, and so a vicious circle may be established in countries battling against poverty. On the optimistic assumptions of fertility decline, the number of children under the age of 15 in the less developed regions of the world, which at present is around 1,100 million, will reach 2,000 million by the end of the century. If present fertility rates continue, their numbers will exceed 2,500 million. On either assumption, an enormous social investment will be called for, often in countries where welfare services are already meagre and governments hard-pressed to maintain them at their present level. Can the countries concerned produce the capital needed for this commitment, with enough to spare for economic development? If the increase in national output resulting from the larger labour force is sufficiently great, the growing population can, in effect, pay for itself. If not, the demands of demographic investment will impose sacrifices in other fields.

In some respects the prospect is not encouraging. The number of illiterate adults in the world is rising by about 4 million a year, and this in spite of the remarkable success of the developing nations in expanding educational facilities to cater for the growing numbers of children knocking on the school doors—the trouble here is that, once their schooling is over, many adults fall back into illiteracy. Again, the number of hospital beds available to the population, already desperately low in most developing countries, has often failed to keep ahead of the rising tide, notwithstanding the determined efforts of governments to expand medical facilities. With few exceptions, the housing conditions of the mass of the people get grimmer every day, over large areas of the Third World. Unemployment is rife.

The Minister of Finance and Economic Planning for Ghana described the situation in blunt terms when his Government decided to launch a national family planning programme in May 1971, saying: "Our rate of population growth far exceeds the rate of growth of our economy. In simple terms, it means that we are increasing faster than we can build schools to educate our youth [. . .] and faster than we can develop our economy to provide jobs for the new workers who enter our labour force each year."

In many ways the problems are more formidable in the cities, in others they press harder on the land. In principle, it is easier to provide schools and hospitals in urban areas, but these advantages are offset by appalling living conditions and mass unemployment. Fast as the world's population is expanding, that of its cities is expanding faster, as millions of impoverished countrymen trek in from the fields in search of the imagined benefits of town life. In the 1920s, 45 million people migrated from the country to the towns; in the 1930s, 90 million made the same one-way journey, and in the 1950s, the great exodus from the land swelled to 170 million, or the equivalent of the entire population of, say, the United States at that time. The total for the 1960s was certainly higher. At the present time, something like 90,000 people move into the towns *every day*—more than 30 million a year. These figures are for the world as a whole. The present urban population of the Third World is about 650 million. By the end of the century it is expected to approach 2,200 million, an increase that is equivalent to more than three times the present population of Europe.

THE KEY QUESTION

Not everybody is alarmed by the population boom. There is, indeed, a respectable body of opinion which holds that, in certain countries at least, a substantial expansion of the population is in the long-term national interest. It cannot be denied that virtually every country in the world has raised economic output in recent years at a faster rate than population growth, and in many cases at a much faster rate. Mexico, for example, has one of the fastest-growing populations in the world, with an annual increase during the First United Nations Development Decade of about 3.6 per cent (see figure 4). In fact, its population grew from 36 million in 1960 to 51 million in 1970. During the same 10 years the national product developed at an average annual rate of 7.1 per cent, so that the income per head still grew by about 3.5 per cent per annum. At that rate it would double every 20 years. While it is a fact that in practice only a privileged minority benefited from this progress, with the mass of the people remaining in the same penurious state as before, it can be argued that this is a problem of income distribution, which admittedly ought to be tackled but which is not necessarily related to high fertility.

Mexico is not a supporter of family planning.[1] Kenya, which is, and which has a population growing almost as fast as Mexico's, also maintained an economic growth rate of about 7 per cent a year in the 1960s. The great majority of developing countries, in fact, attained the First Development Decade target of a 5 per cent annual rate of economic growth. Many comfortably surpassed it, and those which fell short usually did so by small margins. Since none of them had a population growing at significantly more than 3.5 per cent, it can be argued that these figures give no cause for alarm.

Effective economic demand depends, among other things, on the existence of a sufficient number of consumers, living in a sufficiently concentrated community to justify the costs of distribution. The governments of thinly populated countries occupying vast land areas may well feel that these conditions cannot be met, in their case, without a considerable population increase. As they see it,

---

[1] Note that early in 1973, after this book was written, Mexico introduced a national family planning programme within the Ministry of Health.

Figure 4. Growth of population over 25 years at different rates

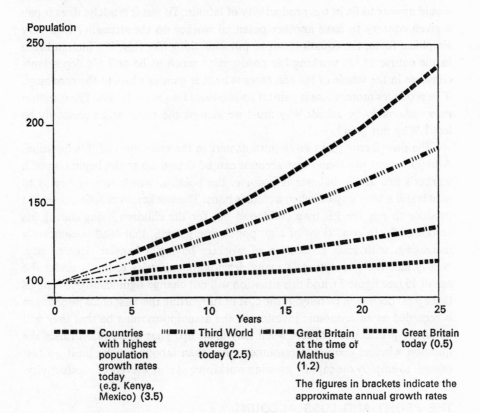

Population

Years

- ▬▬▬ Countries with highest population growth rates today (e.g. Kenya, Mexico) (3.5)
- ▬▬▬ Third World average today (2.5)
- ▬▬▬ Great Britain at the time of Malthus (1.2)
- ▬▬▬ Great Britain today (0.5)

The figures in brackets indicate the approximate annual growth rates

a bigger population would permit the benefits of large-scale production to be enjoyed, and at the same time it would bring transport and communications problems within economic bounds. The same benefits would accrue to the social services, since the cost of schools and hospitals may be prohibitive if they are not within reach of a sufficient number of taxpayers. That being so, many of the leaders of such communities believe that the pressures and hardships caused by rapid population growth should be endured as part of the price to be paid in our time for the well-being of future generations. To advocate family limitation as an aid to economic development is, in their view, to put the cart before the horse. So long as national production is rising faster than population, living standards are bound to rise in time, and so, if European experience is any guide, birth rates are certain sooner or later to fall.

It is rather like the riddle of the chicken and the egg. With every additional mouth to feed, there does come, after all, an additional pair of hands to till the soil or operate a machine when childhood is over. The clue to the problem would appear to lie in the productivity of labour. To put it crudely, does it pay a given country to have another potential worker on the strength? In a very simplified form, the equation can be put something like this: if a human being in the course of his working life produces as much as he and his dependants consume in the whole of his life, there is neither gain nor loss to the economy; if he produces more, there is gain; if he produces less, there is loss. The question may reasonably be asked: why must we assume the result will necessarily be loss? Why not gain?

The time factor plays an important part in the resolution of this question. A hypothetical profit-and-loss account can be drawn up at the beginning of a worker's life. If the balance is positive, the point at which society begins to gain is still a long way off when a child is born. The worker, in practice, does not produce to pay for his own childhood but for the children living during his working life. In conditions of high population growth, that load is constantly increasing, with each generation of workers having a heavier debt to pay. Nearly half the population in many developing countries today is under the age of 15 (see figure 5), and this situation will not change significantly so long as there is no decline in fertility. If the cost of supporting this vast child population is regarded as an economic investment, the assumption must be that they will be highly productive workers when they grow up. That assumption raises the question whether economic resources other than labour can be built up fast enough to employ the rapidly growing workforce at rising levels of productivity.

THE PROFIT-AND-LOSS ACCOUNT

Several attempts have been made to calculate the investment to which a given society is committed by the birth of a child, in terms of food consumption, educational costs, and so on, and to compare this with what might be called the dividend on the investment—the individual's lifetime production, less what he consumes himself. This can then be compared with the returns that might be expected from a similar sum invested over a similar period in some other way—in industry or agriculture, for example. Where there is a national family planning service, the average cost of averting a birth can also be regarded as an investment, the gain or loss on which could be worked out, after a fashion, on the same lines. These calculations make the extreme assumption that all the resources committed to a child's upbringing would in fact be used for investment rather than for consumption if the child had not been born, and are in any case open to the objection that the evaluation of a human life cannot be, or at least ought not to be, placed on the same footing as that of a railway locomotive or a combine harvester.

Figure 5. Population structure by age-group : high fertility and low fertility country

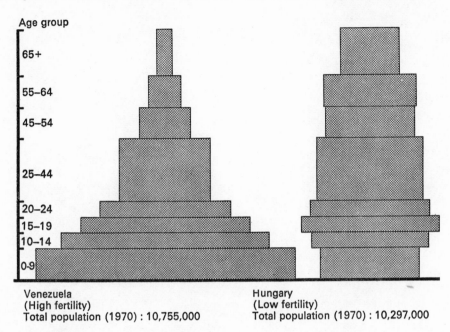

Age group

65+

55–64

45–54

25–44

20–24
15–19
10–14

0-9

Venezuela
(High fertility)
Total population (1970) : 10,755,000

Hungary
(Low fertility)
Total population (1970) : 10,297,000

Source : United Nations Population Division statistics.

Too much should not be made of this type of calculation. After all, in the end, the case most widely put forward against national family planning policies is not economic (though economic arguments may be adduced in its support): it is moral, cultural, and in some cases political. The pros and cons of this wider debate lie outside the scope of the present review. It is for nations, communities, families and individuals to take their stand on the issue, on the strength of their respective convictions and interests.

Let us now look briefly at some of the developing countries whose governments have made up their minds that a population policy is for their people's good, and then take a quick glance at the position in some other countries whose governments are not convinced.

Figure 5. Population structure by age-group, high fertility and low fertility country

THE NATIONAL REACTION

3

The governments of something like 35 developing countries have now adopted family planning programmes. Between them they represent approximately two-thirds of the population of the Third World. Their object is not solely to turn the population tide. A couple who want to have children have just as much right to assistance as a couple wishing to limit their family (it should not be overlooked that 5 per cent of married women have difficulty in conceiving a first child). One of the most important objects of government family planning centres, which are often run in conjunction with the maternity and infant welfare services, is to improve the health of mothers and babies and, through them, that of the community as a whole. In that way, they may even tend to increase potential fertility. None the less, stemming the population flood is in many cases a prime aim of the governments concerned.

THE INDIAN EXPERIENCE

The first country to launch a family planning service as part of its development policy was India, whose First Five-Year Plan (1951-56) incorporated a programme of pilot projects, on the strength of which a nation-wide service was introduced during the Second Five-Year Plan (1956-61). By mid-1969 nearly 28,000 family planning centres and subcentres were in operation and 28 staff training centres had been set up, in which more than 50,000 medical and paramedical personnel had taken courses. If the objectives of the current Fourth Five-Year Plan (1969-74) are attained, by mid-1974 the number of family planning centres should have been raised to 42,000, the number of staff training centres to 51 and of trained staff to more than 200,000. In addition, 1,000 mobile units should be operating from some 300 district offices.

What has been achieved? The population of India at the beginning of the First Plan in 1951 was 356 million; it rose to 445 million in 1961 and to an estimated 570 million in 1971. The birth rate remained fairly constant at 41 per 1,000 right through to about 1968; since then it has fallen to about 39. The object is to bring it down to 32 by the end of the Fourth Plan in 1974 and to 25 by about 1980. When anticipated reductions in death rates have been set against these figures, they imply that the present population growth rate of about 2.7 per cent can be cut to 1.7 per cent by 1980, and with continued progress may average 1.2 per cent over the following 20 years. On these assumptions the population of India will be 300 million less at the end of the century than it might have been if there had been no fall in fertility rates. In fact, it will be about 900 million instead of a possible 1,200 million—three mouths to feed instead of four.

By the middle of 1969 just under 10 million persons in India had either been sterilised or were using contraceptives of one kind or another. The estimated female population "at risk"—in this case taken as the number of married women aged 15 to 49—was just above 100 million, so it appears that roughly one couple in ten were practising birth control. The total number of conceptions prevented during the previous year (the births would, of course, have occurred later) was estimated at about 2.75 million. In the first year of the programme (1956-57) the number was put at less than 11,000.

The total births prevented between the beginning of the programme and approximately the middle of 1969 exceeded 10 million. By the end of the Fourth Plan, in mid-1974, it is expected that 28 million couples in all will be protected and another 18 million births will have been averted. It must be remembered that eventually a multiplier effect begins, as the unborn millions would themselves be having children in the next generation.

A good deal of publicity has been attracted by the part played by voluntary sterilisation in the Indian programme. This minor operation, harmless in itself, is essentially a way of helping couples who already have large families and who have finally decided they do not want bigger ones. The records show that the average client is a man of 35 with five surviving children. Sterilisation is expected to remain an important feature of the Indian programme for many years, but obviously its role is bound to diminish if younger couples succeed in limiting their families. Sterilisation, indeed, is not so much a family planning success as an expedient dictated by the failure of family planning in the past. The same may be said of abortion, which was finally legalised in India at the beginning of 1972. It was estimated that 4 million Indian women a year were having recourse to back-street abortionists.

The average cost to the Indian authorities of preventing a birth is estimated at about 100 rupees, or the equivalent of about $13.

PAKISTAN

Pakistan also began a family planning programme in a small way in its Second Five-Year Plan (1961-65). The Third Five-Year Plan (1965-70) started with the ambitious aim of reducing the birth rate from between 50 and 60 per 1,000 to 40 per 1,000 in the five-year period. At the core of the plan was the training of some 30,000 village midwives to provide family planning advice. In addition, some 1,500 female doctors and health visitors and some 900 family planning officers were to receive short courses. The midwives were paid a small monthly fee for their extra duties, plus a modest sum for each case referred by them to the clinic.

By the middle of 1969 some 4.7 million Pakistanis were practising some sort of birth control. Set against an estimated female population "at risk" of rather more than 19 million, this meant that about a quarter of Pakistani couples at that time were attempting to limit their families. An estimated 3 million births were prevented during the Plan period and the birth rate came down to 43 per 1,000. The goals of the Fourth Five-Year Plan (1970-75) were to reduce the birth rate to 33.2 per 1,000 and prevent a further 9.6 million births. Since then the secession of Bangladesh has affected the national statistics.

KENYA

The first African country south of the Sahara to enter the field in a determined way was Kenya, a country of about 10.5 million inhabitants at the 1969 census. With a birth rate of 50 per 1,000 and a death rate of 17 per 1,000, Kenya's population is growing at 3.3 per cent per annum. At this rate, a population doubles every 21 years. The Government of Kenya launched a national family planning programme in 1967 in co-operation with the Family Planning Association of Kenya.

The Kenya programme is a free service operated as part of the National Health Service, with family planning facilities provided at all the country's hospitals, health centres and dispensaries. This means that there are, in effect, some 800 birth control clinics, with a further 150 under construction. Seven mobile teams operate in the more remote areas. In support of this effort the Family Planning Association employs about 50 field educators, who tour the country explaining the benefits of family planning and drawing attention to the services the clinics can provide.

As in India and Pakistan, the Government of Kenya regards the family planning programme as an integral part of the nation's social and economic development plans. No specific targets have been set, the Government being content to aim at the fastest possible reduction of the country's natural growth rate that can be achieved by voluntary action. There are therefore no estimates of prevented births, but the numbers of women attending the clinics is steadily rising. In the first year (1967) some 1,500 made first visits, in the second some 11,700, in the third over 30,000, and in the first half of 1970 the figure was more than 16,700, or an annual rate of 33,000. Thus by mid-1970 some 60,000 women had been to the clinics and the great majority of them had adopted contraception. This figure represents about 1 in 35 of the country's 2.1 million married women of child-bearing age—by no means a slow start.

NORTHERN AFRICA

In northern Africa three countries (Morocco, Egypt and Tunisia) have official population policies. The aim of the Moroccan Government is to reduce the crude birth rate from about 50 per 1,000, which was the level at the beginning of the 1968-72 Development Plan, to 45 per 1,000 by 1972 and to 35 per 1,000 in 1985. By 1971 it was estimated that about 150,000 Moroccan women, or 1 in 20 of child-bearing age, were using either the national family planning service or privately obtained contraceptives. In 1969 Egypt adopted a target of reducing the birth rate, which was then about 45 per 1,000, by a point per year for the following ten years. Nearly 3,000 family planning clinics are in operation, and about 10 per cent of Egyptian women of child-bearing age were using either public or private contraceptive supplies in 1971. The longest established of the three services in northern Africa is that of Tunisia, where the number of married couples using the national service was estimated at 9 per cent at the beginning of 1971, with a further 3 per cent obtaining supplies from commercial sources. The Tunisian target is a birth rate of 38 per 1,000 in 1976, reduced from a level of about 45 per 1,000 at the beginning of the decade. With more than 300 centres and 14 mobile units, the Tunisian family planning service currently reports about 30,000 new clients a year, and the numbers are steadily increasing. The total includes some 2,500 sterilisations and about the same number of abortions. Women who already have five or more children may obtain an abortion on request.

THE MIDDLE EAST

Two countries in the Middle East—Iran and Turkey—have official population policies. The older is that of Turkey, which dates back to a law passed in April 1965, the first provision of which states that individuals may have as many children as they wish, whenever they wish, and that this can be ensured through preventive measures taken against pregnancy; however, neither castration, sterilisation nor the termination of pregnancy may be performed unless medically necessary. The regulations subsequently adopted were such that most women desiring an abortion can in practice generally obtain one under medical care. Before the introduction of the regulations, an estimated 200,000 abortions

were being performed annually in Turkey, at least 150,000 of which were illegal. In most areas of the country it seems that the women wish to limit their families, and there is generally no opposition from the husbands. A survey in the early 1960s revealed that the average number of children wanted by Turkish women was 3.2, while in 1970 the average household in western Turkey contained 4.7 persons and in eastern Turkey 8.5 persons. These figures include adults, but on the other hand the "average" mother would be only halfway through her child-bearing years.

The aim of the Family Planning Division of the Turkish Ministry of Health is to bring services to an additional 5 per cent of all women of child-bearing age each year, or about 350,000 women per annum. Each of Turkey's 67 provinces has a family planning director, who may be a gynaecologist or the provincial medical officer of health. Some 500 clinics have been established. Mobile teams, normally consisting of two vehicles, operate in the remote areas. The first vehicle carries one male and one female educator, who hold meetings in the villages; the second follows a day later with a doctor and a midwife, who provide family planning services. In addition, the monthly bulletin of the Family Planning Division is sent to the headmen of about 12,000 villages, where it is often read aloud. By 1970 the number of women using the national family planning service was growing by about 70,000 a year and the cumulative total was about 300,000. Turkey has not published estimates of prevented births, but the authorities are confident that the programme will gather momentum.

In Iran the aim is to reduce the population growth rate from 3 per cent to 2 per cent per annum. A feature of this programme is the intensive educational activity in which volunteer organisations like the Literacy Corps, the Women's Corps, the Health Corps, the Development Corps and the co-operative societies are engaged. Up to the end of 1969 between 30,000 and 40,000 members of these bodies had received family planning training. In January 1971 the Iranian family planning service reported upwards of 375,000 regular users, to which could be added an estimated 75,000 couples who were making use of commercial sources. The female population aged 15 to 44 at that time was about 5.6 million. The Ministry of Health maintains 512 permanent centres and 350 mobile clinics operating in the remote areas. In addition, the army has 22 clinics. Sterilisation is illegal, but abortion is permitted on medical grounds. Recent returns showed that 20 per cent of all patients admitted to the Farah Maternity Hospital in Teheran were suffering from the effects of self-induced abortion.

LATIN AMERICA

Family planning programmes are being introduced in an increasing number of Latin American countries. Few countries have an *official* population policy, but this does not necessarily imply opposition to family planning services provided by non-government agencies and indeed by the state medical service on health grounds. In its publication *Family planning in five continents*, the International Planned Parenthood Federation lists the following States among those with government-supported family planning programmes: Chile, Colombia, Costa Rica, Dominican Republic, El Salvador, Guatemala, Honduras, Nicaragua, Panama and Venezuela. In practice, the difference between those nations whose governments are committed to family planning programmes and those supporting family limitation in the interests of the mothers' and children's health (such as Bolivia and Ecuador) is essentially one of approach. There may be no propaganda campaigns in support of national population control, but the actual provision of family planning services may be as extensive as in countries in the anti-natalist camp. Widespread publicity may indeed be given to the service, on health and welfare grounds.

In Chile family planning has been incorporated in the National Health Service since 1966, and a new Ministry of Family Protection was established towards the end of 1970. By that time more than 1,200 persons had been specifically allocated to the family planning services, including 360 doctors and 480 midwives. The number of hospitals and clinics providing the service exceeded 350. The record of attendance is higher than that of many countries pursuing official population policies. By the end of 1969 more than 500,000 women had visited the centres for contraceptive advice, and while the numbers continuing to practise birth control techniques are not reported they would presumably be in the majority. On any showing, they represent a high proportion of the female population of child-bearing age, which in Chile in 1970 totalled just over 2 million.

The vigour with which the authorities promote the service may be gauged from the fact that a target of a 35 per cent increase in clinical activities over the previous year was set for 1970. Sex education is conducted by the Family Planning Association, an affiliate of the International Planned Parenthood Federation.

Colombia has 400 centres, 3 mobile teams, 80 doctors working full time and more than 1,000 working part time in the family planning service, plus 500 village health promoters and a paramedical staff of more than 300. Up to the end of 1970 more than 300,000 Colombian women had attended the centres out of approximately 4 million of child-bearing age. As in Chile, the Family Planning Association runs regular courses in sex education.

Chile and Colombia are fairly typical of the situation in Latin America, where, contrary to widespread belief, family planning is by no means universally condemned. Even in countries which advocate population expansion, such as Argentina and Brazil, the family planning activities of voluntary organisations are generally allowed on health and welfare grounds. The International

Planned Parenthood Federation has in fact national affiliates in these countries. The Mexican affiliate, the Foundation for Population Studies, operates 50 family planning clinics which provided services in 1970 to more than 180,000 persons, an increase of over 75 per cent over the previous year.

There is a good deal of evidence that personal motivation is fairly strong in Latin America. An inquiry among Catholic women in seven national capitals revealed that more than half of them had used some form of contraception after they had borne two children and that more than three-quarters had done so after they had borne four children. In Argentina an interesting aspect of this survey was the relatively high figure for Buenos Aires, the richest of the Latin American capitals, where more than 40 per cent of married Catholic women had used some contraception technique before they had borne a child, and 80 per cent who had borne one child had attempted at some time, or were then attempting, to prevent the birth of a second. These results were published in 1966. Another study published in the same year revealed that 95 per cent of mothers in Brazil who already had three children did not want a fourth. In Colombia the figure was 67 per cent, in Costa Rica 67 per cent, in Mexico 64 per cent and in Panama 70 per cent. This was at a time when family planning services were meagre or non-existent in most parts of Latin America.

CHINA

China links a planned population policy with a planned social production policy, supporting family planning in the interests of mothers and children. China accepts the classical Marxist analysis of the issue, which was first stated by Karl Marx himself in his well-known reply to Robert Malthus in *Das Kapital*. Malthus had argued in his famous *Essay on population* in 1798 that if Britain's population (then doubling about every 50 years) were not restrained by late marriage and continence the population would outstrip the means of production. Marx replied, in effect, that this appeared to be the case only because labour was steadily being displaced by machinery; productive capacity was in fact expanding faster than population, but much of it was machine capacity and as a result many of the increased population were condemned to idleness and hunger. He concluded that in a scientifically planned economy, where labour and capital were not rival forces but were both equally at the disposal of the community, this contradiction would disappear.

The head of the Chinese delegation to the 1972 United Nations Conference on the Human Environment, Tang Ke, took up much the same position in his address to the Conference, saying: "The history of mankind has proved that the pace of development of production, science and technology always surpasses by far the rate of population growth. The possibility of man's exploitation and utilisation of natural resources is inexhaustible. [. . .] Of course, this in no way means that we approve of the unchecked growth of population. Our Government has always approved of family planning. But it is wholly groundless to think that population growth in itself will give rise to poverty and backwardness."

In 1957 Chairman Mao compared the country's rate of population growth with the needs of food production and of educational facilities. Though the grain harvest had been growing by 10 million tons a year, he said that this was "barely sufficient to cover the needs of our growing population," adding: "Steps must therefore be taken to keep our population for a long time at a stable level." The previous year the Ministry of Health had announced that "contraception is a democratic right of the people; [. . .] the Government should provide every condition possible to guide the masses and meet their needs for contraception." In 1964 Premier Chou En-lai set a target of a 1 per cent annual population growth rate by the end of the century (the present rate is believed to be about 2 per cent).[1]

In 1950 the legal minimum marrying age in China was raised to 18 for women and 20 for men. The recommended minimum is now 25 for women and 30 for men. This is not enforced by law, but public esteem is bestowed upon the couple who postpone marriage to the recommended years. Chinese women may obtain an abortion on request up to two-and-a-half months after conception, though they are not encouraged to regard this as an alternative to contraception. The same is true of sterilisation, which may be requested by either husband or wife. The contraceptive pill is distributed free, and is manufactured in what is believed to be the largest chain of laboratories for this purpose in the world. None the less, the supply apparently still falls short of demand.

JAPAN

Some industrialised countries support family planning for health reasons without proclaiming a national population policy. One of the most remarkable of these is Japan where, as we saw above, the birth rate fell from 34 per 1,000 in 1947 to 17 per 1,000 only ten years later. Legalised abortion played an important part in the early stages of this downward trend, but contraception is now practised by the great majority of married couples[2], notwithstanding a ban on the contraceptive pill. The Eugenic Protection Law of 1948 was introduced to safeguard the health of women by legalising abortion on medical grounds. At that time clandestine abortion was widespread in Japan, as indeed it still is through

---

[1] Chairman Mao's and Premier Chou En-lai's remarks are quoted in *Population and family planning in the People's Republic of China* (Washington, DC, Victor-Bostrom Fund, 1971).

[2] The proportion increased from 20 per cent in 1950 to 68 per cent by 1961.

the greater part of the world. (Just how widespread, of course, cannot be known.) The year after the law was passed in Japan 100,000 abortions were carried out and four years later a million were performed. Medical opinion began to fear that women's health might be damaged by repeated abortions, and in consequence the Government, in 1965, enacted the Maternal and Child Health Law, under which birth control advice may be provided as a means of avoiding recourse to abortion. This was accompanied by an appropriate propaganda campaign.

A curious feature of Japanese law is that, whereas the contraceptive pill is banned, sterilisation has been legalised since the adoption of the 1948 Eugenic Protection Law—the exact reverse of the position in many countries. About 40,000 sterilisations are in fact performed every year. A tantalising question is how much of the remarkable decline in fertility in Japan is a consequence of changes in the law and how much is the effect of differences in social behaviour resulting from the extraordinary pace of economic development (average incomes in Japan quadrupled between 1958 and 1968).

THE MAIN DIFFICULTY

The main difficulty facing governments, both those committed to population control and those advocating population expansion, is still in most cases the lack of sufficiently strong motivation on the part of couples. The wish but not the will is there. The efforts of several European countries to pursue population policies with the hope of boosting the supposedly dwindling national stock have nowhere met with resounding success. Every kind of encouragement may be offered for larger families—children's allowances, tax concessions, exemption from military service, travel concessions on the state transport system, patriotic acclaim—to little apparent effect. Most married couples in Europe have simply decided they would be happier with small families.

Similarly, where the desire to limit child-bearing has been awakened, pessimism about the practical possibilities often persists notwithstanding what has been achieved to date. In countries offering official family planning facilities there are undoubtedly large numbers of women who still stay away because they are not convinced that the clinic can do much more for them than they can do for themselves. Yet when the news spread in India that the welfare centres were offering a "new" method which was apparently trouble-free over a long period (the inter-uterine device or "IUD"), remarkable scenes were witnessed in some of the villages. The following extract is taken from a 1966 United Nations mission report on the family planning programme in India: "When a trial with the device was started in Madurai, Madras, women in rural areas stopped the city hospital's ambulance on the road to ask for the device. During a similar trial at the Lady Hardinge Hospital, New Delhi, the demand became so heavy that the doors had to be closed and some clients were turned away. [. . .] In a recent article in *Yojana* (June 1965) it was reported that the dissemination of detailed information on this method in one or two villages near New Delhi resulted in women from neighbouring villages flocking in and requesting services."

These poor people had probably in many cases already had several children, for except in the most sophisticated societies the evidence everywhere suggests that family limitation is not seriously attempted, as a rule, until a couple have had the children they desire. Many years of possible child-bearing may then remain, especially where girls marry young. Hence most couples will still have at least one unplanned birth through carelessness or failure. Spacing the births from the beginning of marriage is the true meaning of family planning. It is also the way to heighten the happiness of childhood and the joys of parenthood.

INTERNATIONAL CONCERN

4

The first world population conference was convened privately in 1927. Albert Thomas, the first Director of the International Labour Office, addressed the conference in his personal capacity, but neither the League of Nations nor the ILO was represented officially. This conference was not, in fact, concerned with rapid population growth. The populations of most of the countries represented were growing slowly and their growth rates, already low, were expected to continue in decline. Few of the 123 experts came from what we now think of as the developing world. Some of them pointed out that populations in the economically more backward regions would expand as death rates began to fall, but mostly they assumed that this expansion would be of relatively short duration, and that the pattern they had observed in Europe would fairly quickly assert itself everywhere. Others were content to leave famine, war and disease to regulate the situation. Rapid population growth was not a matter of world concern at that time.

After the Second World War the extreme delicacy of the subject prevented the United Nations from taking the initiative until relatively late in the day, notwithstanding the establishment of the Population Commission of the Economic and Social Council as early as 1946. Some assistance was given at the request of member States, including advice on family planning, and a United Nations world population conference was in fact held in Rome in 1954 in collaboration with the International Union for the Scientific Study of Population, for the purpose of pooling scientific views and experience: but no resolutions or recommendations for action were discussed. Generally speaking, therefore, demographic problems waited in the wings until 1962, when the issue first came before the General Assembly in the form of a resolution on population growth and economic development.

THE GENERAL ASSEMBLY RESOLUTION, 1962

The 1962 General Assembly resolution requested the Secretary-General to conduct an inquiry among governments and the specialised agencies of the United Nations concerning the particular problems confronting them as a result of the reciprocal action of economic development and population changes. It also recommended that the Population Commission should intensify its studies and research on the interrelationship of population growth and economic and social development, with particular reference to the needs of the developing countries for investment in health and educational facilities within the framework of their general development programmes.

A clause recommending that the United Nations should give technical assistance, as requested by governments, for national projects and programmes dealing with the problems of population, narrowly failed to be adopted, the voting being 34 for and 34 against, with 32 abstentions. The opponents of this clause were not necessarily opposed to family planning or even to national population policies; they included delegations which simply held that, whatever the merits or demerits of population planning might be, it was not an appropriate field for United Nations action. Others who abstained held that the clause was superfluous, since the United Nations already had authority to give technical assistance in any field at the request of member States.

The ensuing inquiry elicited responses from 55 governments, several of which held that rapid population growth did not present a problem in their countries, which they considered were, if anything, too thinly inhabited. Others, however, saw a need for action. An Asian population conference, held in New Delhi in December 1963 under the auspices of the United Nations Economic Commission for Asia and the Far East, requested the United Nations and specialised agencies to expand the scope of technical assistance available to governments in the region, upon their request, for data collection, research, experimentation and action in all aspects of population problems, including family welfare planning programmes. Encouraged by this initiative, a United Nations advisory mission visited India in 1965 to examine that country's family planning programme at the Government's request. This was the first operation of its kind undertaken by the United Nations.

THE WORLD POPULATION CONFERENCE, 1965

In the same year the second World Population Conference was held at Belgrade on the initiative of the Population Commission. On this occasion a large number of specialists from countries at various levels of development took part. The highlights of the Conference were summarised in a United Nations publication with the significant title, *World population: challenge to development*. The following year, at its 21st Session, the General Assembly adopted a key resolution on population growth and economic development, in which the appropriate United Nations organs and the specialised agencies were invited to study the proceedings of the World Population Conference. In this resolution the General Assembly recognised the sovereignty of nations in executing their own population policies, with due regard to the principle that the size of the family should be the free choice of each individual family.

Finally, the 1966 resolution called upon the United Nations, the regional economic commissions and the specialised agencies to assist, when requested, in further developing and strengthening national and regional facilities for training, research, information and advisory services in the field of population, bearing in mind the different character of population problems in each country and region and the needs arising therefrom. This 1966 resolution of the General Assembly was adopted unanimously.

THE INTERNATIONAL CONFERENCE ON HUMAN RIGHTS, 1968

On Human Rights Day, 1966, the Secretary-General received a manifesto signed by 12 Heads of State proclaiming the basic human right of individuals to determine the number and spacing of their children. The following year this pronouncement was signed by a further 18 Heads of State and was officially presented to the Secretary-General at a ceremony at United Nations headquarters, with the title "World Leaders' Declaration on Population".[1] The substance of this declaration was subsequently adopted by the United Nations International Conference on Human Rights, held at Teheran in 1968, in a resolution on the human rights aspects of family planning. This resolution observes that "the present rapid rate of population growth in some areas of the world hampers the struggle against hunger and poverty, and in particular reduces the possibilities of rapidly achieving adequate standards of living, including food, clothing, housing, medical care, social security, education and social services, thereby impairing the full realisation of human rights". It couples with the right to decide the number and spacing of children the "right to adequate education and information in this respect". The principle recurs in the "Proclamation of Teheran", adopted unanimously at the end of the Conference: "Parents have a basic human right to determine freely and responsibly the number and spacing of their children."

---

[1] The signatories were the Heads of State or Prime Ministers of Australia, Barbados, Colombia, Denmark, Dominican Republic, Finland, Ghana, India, Indonesia, Iran, Japan, Jordan, Republic of Korea, Malaysia, Morocco, Nepal, Netherlands, New Zealand, Norway, Pakistan, Philippines, Singapore, Sweden, Thailand, Trinidad and Tobago, Tunisia, United Arab Republic (now Egypt), United Kingdom, United States and Yugoslavia. They spoke for more than one-third of the world's people.

THE DECLARATION ON SOCIAL PROGRESS AND DEVELOPMENT, 1969

In 1969 the General Assembly adopted the Declaration on Social Progress and Development, a comprehensive document containing 27 articles. Many of these articles reaffirm and develop the principles embodied in the Universal Declaration of Human Rights and in various international covenants and conventions, but article 22 broke new ground by listing three of the objectives of social progress as being: (1) the development and co-ordination of policies and measures designed to strengthen the essential functions of the family as a basic unit of society; (2) the formulation and establishment, as needed, of programmes in the field of population, including "the provision to families of the knowledge and means necessary to enable them to exercise their right to determine freely and responsibly the number and spacing of their children"; and (3) the establishment of appropriate child-care facilities in the interest of children and working parents.

Meanwhile, the First United Nations Development Decade was drawing to a close, and the Second Development Decade was about to be launched. A certain disappointment with the achievements of the First Development Decade, notwithstanding the impressive national economic growth rates attained in many countries, led to the incorporation of demographic objectives in the strategy of the Second Development Decade. Thus, an economic growth rate of about 3.5 per cent per head per year was set up as a target for developing countries, and member States were enjoined to formulate appropriate demographic objectives within the framework of national development plans.

The International Development Strategy for the Second United Nations Development Decade states: "Those developing countries which consider that their rate of population growth hampers their development will adopt measures which they deem necessary in accordance with their concept of development. Developed countries, consistent with their national policies, will, upon request, provide support through supply of means for family planning and further research. International organisations concerned will continue to provide, when appropriate, the assistance that may be requested by interested governments. Such support or assistance will not be a substitute for other forms of development assistance."

WORLD POPULATION YEAR, 1974

The year 1974, approximately halfway through the Second Development Decade, has been designated as World Population Year. This was resolved by the General Assembly at its 25th Session in 1970. In an annex to his report to the Population Commission in November 1971, the Secretary-General explained the broad purpose of this decision in the following words: "On the occasion of the World Population Year, 1974, the governments and the peoples of the world must consider the great social and economic anomalies which persist despite pledges by nations to devote themselves to humanitarian ideals of economic and social progress and better standards of life, and despite intellectual and technical achievements in space, communications, agriculture, medicine and other fields. In spite of these significant achievements, great individual and national inequalities in wealth persist at the international level and within nations of every stage of development, as a consequence of maladjustments between demographic, social, economic and environmental factors. Growing individual and group tensions are to be found both within and between nations. Not only has the quality of life failed to improve at desirable rates, but there are new and different fears that the future is increasingly menaced by population growth and structural change, accompanied by environmental deterioration and, in the developing countries, by delay in the application of scientific and technical knowledge."

A highlight of the World Population Year will be the third United Nations World Population Conference, to be held at United Nations headquarters in August 1974. The conferences of 1954 and 1965 were essentially scientific gatherings carried out in collaboration with the International Union for the Scientific Study of Population. The 1974 meeting, however, will be devoted to basic demographic problems and their relationship with economic and social development.[1] The appropriate agencies of the United Nations are co-operating in the preparation of background papers in their specialised fields, and every member State will be invited to submit a statement on national population trends in relation to development policy in its own country. This invitation will be extended to nations that are members of certain specialised agencies without belonging to the United Nations itself.

THE UNITED NATIONS FUND FOR POPULATION ACTIVITIES

Since 1967 a separate fund, the United Nations Fund for Population Activities, has been in existence to finance technical assistance in the population field, as well as approved projects such as studies and reports on different

---

[1] Five major topics will be discussed: (1) recent population trends and future prospects; (2) relations between population change and economic and social development; (3) relations between population, resources and environment; (4) population and the family; (5) a draft World Population Plan of Action.

aspects of the problem. Like the Special Fund of the United Nations Development Programme, UNFPA is financed by voluntary contributions from member States. At the same time, while there has never been much doubt as to the right of United Nations organisations to provide technical co-operation in this field at a government's request, most of the leading agencies passed specific conference resolutions in the 1960s making it clear that they were willing to help with demographic and family planning activities. The World Health Organization did so in 1965, the International Labour Organisation, the Food and Agriculture Organization and the United Nations Children's Fund in 1967, and the World Bank and Unesco in 1968.

THE ILO AND POPULATION [1]

The ILO has been concerned with population growth since long before the 1967 resolution just mentioned, by virtue of its preoccupation with vocational training, workers' welfare and above all the scourge of unemployment. The tripartite structure of the Organisation, in which the representatives of workers' organisations throughout the world have an equal voice with governments and employers, has always meant that the ILO has been quick to feel the pressures disturbing the mass of the people. Thus the major Employment Policy Convention, 1964 (No. 122), which was adopted following several years of discussion, was accompanied by the detailed Employment Policy Recommendation, 1964 (No. 122), outlining the objectives and methods of national employment policy, in which the influence of population growth was specifically recognised. Paragraph 28 of the Recommendation requests countries in which the population is increasing rapidly, and especially those in which it already presses heavily on the economy, to study the economic, social and demographic factors affecting population growth with a view to achieving a better balance between the growth of employment opportunities and the growth of the labour force.

The resolution adopted by the Asian Regional Conference of the ILO in Tokyo in 1968 stressed the strong link between employment planning in Asia and the demographic factor. The resolution urged Asian countries to formulate population policies, where appropriate, and to organise family planning and educational activities for workers' families, in co-operation with trade unions and employers' associations. The ILO, it added, should be authorised to co-operate in these activities. The four major country reports so far produced under the World Employment Programme—for

---

[1] The ILO's activities in the field of population are considered in greater detail in Annex IV.

Colombia, Iran, Kenya and Sri Lanka—dwell on the influence of rapid population growth, and there can be little doubt that the reports of future ILO comprehensive employment strategy missions will do the same. Thus the ILO may be said to have been drawn irresistibly into the deep waters of demographic debate by the very nature of its mandate.

In 1967, the year when the United Nations itself and several of its specialised agencies highlighted the population question in the world forum, the International Labour Conference unanimously adopted the resolution which gave rise to the present survey. The resolution requested the Director-General to investigate the influence and consequences of rapid population growth on opportunities for training and employment and on welfare of workers, and to submit proposals to the Governing Body on the further action that might be taken by the ILO.

The wording of the first part of this request is significant. It refers to *opportunities* for training and employment. This survey is thus concerned with social justice, not merely with economic efficiency, for it could happen that the training facilities of a country were adequate for economic development in a narrow sense, without providing working people with the equal opportunities demanded by the Declaration of Philadelphia and the Constitution of the ILO.

The ILO's main contribution to the Second United Nations Development Decade as regards employment objectives and policies is represented by the World Employment Programme, which has to do with the whole range of development problems as they affect employment. One of the main research projects under the World Employment Programme is concerned with the relationship between population growth and employment, specifically because a decrease in population growth now may have immediate effects on the *demand* for labour—for instance, by making more money available for savings and investment—although obviously the effects on the *size* of the workforce will not come about for at least a decade. As we have already seen, there are many divergent opinions on population matters, and through its research under the World Employment Programme the ILO hopes to shed more light on these controversial issues and to expand our knowledge of the whole subject.

Mass unemployment, lack of training facilities, meagre welfare services, obviously retard the construction of a just society. If it can be shown that these evils are compounded by rapid population growth, then justice—between man and man, between man and woman and between nation and nation—requires that the ILO should look this problem squarely in the face.

THE PROBLEMS

THE PROBLEMS

EDUCATION UNDER STRAIN

5

MILLIONS MORE CHILDREN

One of the first and most obvious effects of rapid population growth is that it places a tremendous strain on a country's educational resources. This is vividly illustrated by the contrasting population pyramids shown in figure 5. And this strain is not likely to be relieved in the foreseeable future: between 1970 and 1985—a mere 15 years—the world total of children under the age of 15 is expected to increase by nearly 450 million, 400 million of whom will be in the Third World. This Third World increase alone, over a period of only 15 years, greatly exceeds the total number of children under 15 years old now living in the whole of the more developed parts of the world, which is estimated at a fraction under 300 million. Indeed, if we look at the projections merely for the ten years of the Second Development Decade, from 1970 to 1980, we find an anticipated increase of approximately 270 million in the number of Third World children under 15 years of age, an increase that exceeds the total number of children under that age living at the present time in the whole of Europe, the Soviet Union, the United States, Canada, Australia and New Zealand combined, currently estimated at about 265 million. At the end of the Decade, approximately two-thirds of all these children will have reached the age when they should be at school, if that age is assumed to be 5 years. If they were to have educational opportunities equal to those of children in more fortunate lands, their governments would, within ten years, have to build, equip and train teachers for as many schools as now exist in the whole of the six regions listed above!

No conceivable change in fertility rates can prevent educational needs from rising steeply in the developing countries for many years to come. In Africa, Latin America and most of Asia today, more than 40 persons out of every 100 are below the age of 15. The contrast with lower fertility countries is very marked: in Europe only 25 persons out of every 100 are under 15; in North America the figure is 30, and in the USSR 29. The average for the more developed regions is in fact about 27 out of every 100. Moreover, in many developing countries little substantial change can be expected in this age distribution in the present century. In western Africa, for example, which is currently the world's most fecund region, there are at present 46 children under the age of 15 for every 100 people, and this proportion—almost half the human stock—is expected to persist right through to the year 2000 and beyond. Indeed, if anything, it is expected to increase slightly as general health and maternity services improve. The same is true of other countries of tropical Africa, where the number of children below the age of 15 varies from about 40 to about 42 per 100 of the population. These are the parts of the world where birth rates are highest and where they are not expected to change significantly in coming years.

In other developing regions some decline in fertility is anticipated—slight in the case of Latin America, more marked in certain other areas. As we saw in Chapter 1, the United Nations population estimates are based on four different fertility assumptions. On the medium assumption, the percentage of children under 15 in the population of China would fall from the present figure of about 35 to approximately 27 by the end of the century; in India and Pakistan from the present 42 to about 33; in the Middle East from 43 to rather more than 37; and in Latin America from 42 to 38. This certainly does not mean, however, that the actual number of children will decline, as these are percentages of rapidly growing total populations. To take but one example, the number of children under 15 years of age in the Indian subcontinent is expected to grow from approximately 320 million in 1970 to 460 million by the close of the century 30 years later, notwithstanding a percentage drop of more than 9 per cent. In western Africa, where no percentage drop is predicted, there will be approximately two-and-a-half times as many children to feed and educate in the year 2000 as there are today.[1]

THE STRUGGLE AGAINST ILLITERACY

As we have already noticed, the number of illiterate adults in the world is increasing by some 4 million a year (see figure 6), notwithstanding the tremendous efforts made by developing countries to expand their educational facilities. Indeed, of the world's less developed regions, it is only in Latin America that the number of adult illiterates has declined in recent years,

---

[1] These calculations are based on the United Nations Population Division's projections published in 1968. As noted in Chapter 1, a new set of projections is now in preparation, but it is not expected that the later figures will show any significant changes in this respect.

Figure 6.   The struggle against illiteracy : world population aged 15 and over

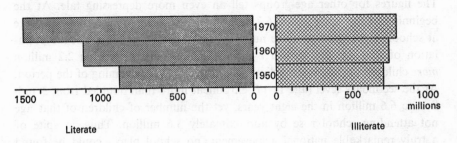

Literate   Illiterate

Source: Unesco: *A summary statistical review of education in the world, 1971* (Paris, 1971).

with a drop from 40 million in 1960 to 38.6 million in 1970. Some impression of the educational investment that this achievement entailed may be gleaned from the fact that between 1950 and 1968 the number of children enrolled in primary schools in Latin America rose from 15 million to 41 million. During the same 18 years it rose from 8.5 million to 29 million in Africa and from 53 million to 133 million in Asia (excluding China); yet in these areas total illiteracy increased, mainly because of population pressure. These figures indicate the magnitude of the task confronting the developing nations.

With population growth placing such a great strain on educational resources, girls tend to find themselves at the back of the queue. In 1960 male illiterates in the world totalled 307 million and female illiterates 428 million. Ten years later, the number of illiterate males had risen by a further 8 million and of illiterate females by a further 40 million—five times as many. Of the total world population over 15 years of age, 40 per cent of the females were unable to read and write in 1970. In most developing countries the proportion of girl students in schools and colleges is rising, if slowly, but they have a long way to go to be on an equal footing with the boys. In primary schools in Africa and Asia there are still six boys enrolled for every four girls. In secondary schools in Africa there are seven boys to three girls, and in Asian secondary schools the ratio is only fractionally more favourable. In Latin America, on the other hand, enrolment of boys and girls is more nearly equal in primary and secondary schools.

The Indian record brings out very clearly the relentless population pressure on a developing country's educational resources. In the school year 1960/61, 35 million children aged 6 to 11 were enrolled in the primary schools of India. Eight years later, the numbers enrolled had risen to no fewer than 56 million, a tremendous achievement on any showing. Yet the number of infants *not* attending school had in fact fallen by less than 6 million (from 21.4 million in 1960 to 15.7 million in 1968), the reason for this being that the population aged 6 to 11 had actually increased during those eight years by 15 million. The figures for other age-groups tell an even more depressing tale. At the beginning of the same period 6.7 million Indian children aged 11 to 14 were at school; eight years later the number had risen by 6 million, but the population of that age had grown by more than 8 million, leaving 2.2 million *more* children outside intermediate school than at the beginning of the period. At the secondary level (age 14-17) enrolment more than doubled from 3 million to 6.6 million in the eight years, yet the number of children of that age not attending school rose by approximately 3.6 million. Thus, in spite of a truly remarkable national achievement, no school places could be found for many millions of the extra Indian children who had come into the world.

A significant feature of the Indian scene, typical of most developing countries, is the small number of children who receive anything more than the most rudimentary schooling. While in the school year 1968/69 roughly four Indian children out of every five aged 6 to 11 were at school, only one in three aged 11 to 14 and only one in five aged 14 to 17 were able to continue their education. In other words, two children out of every three of that generation received no formal education after the age of 11, and four out of five never reached a secondary school (see figure 7). This can only mean that something like 25 million Indian children out of some 37 million aged 11 to 14 at that time were either already working on the family farm, already seeking employment, or wasting their lives.

To meet the targets of India's Fourth Five-Year Plan (1969-74), an additional 464,000 teachers will be required, plus a further 333,000 to replace retired staff, making a teacher-training load of approximately 800,000 in five years. If the Plan succeeds, there will be another 13 million schoolchildren aged 6 to 11, another 6 million aged 11 to 14 and another 3.8 million at secondary school—a bold step forward. Still, three Indian children out of four will have no opportunity of entering a secondary school and the absolute numbers in that age-group not at school will actually have increased again by about 1.5 million. In the 15 years from 1960 to 1974 the population of secondary school age in India will have grown from 27.5 million to approximately 40 million, the numbers attending secondary school from 3.0 million to 10.4 million and the total *not* going to secondary school from 24.5 million to 29.6 million. So everything grows. The population grows. The number of school places grows, and the number of children left outside also grows.

THE EFFECT ON NATIONAL DEVELOPMENT

The diversion of a high proportion of the community's earnings, not only to educate but also to feed, clothe, house and care for such vast numbers

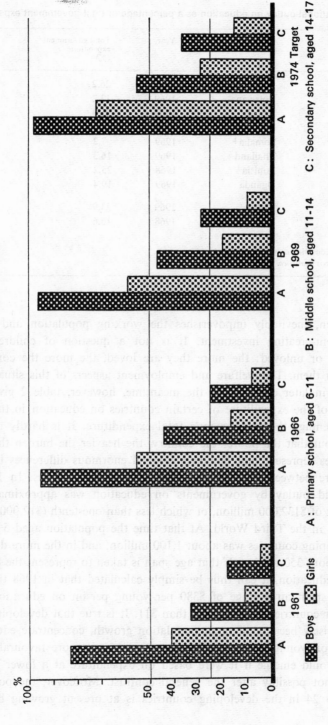

Figure 7. School enrolments in India as a percentage of all children in the relevant age-groups

A : Primary school, aged 6-11   B : Middle school, aged 11-14   C : Secondary school, aged 14-17

■ Boys   ▩ Girls

Source: based on statistics in Government of India: *Fourth Five-Year Plan (1969-74)*.

Table 2. National outlay on education as a percentage of total government expenditure

Country	Year	Total government expenditure (%)
Bolivia	1969	26.2
Botswana	1969	13.2
Ecuador	1969	25.0
Pakistan	1969	5.2
Somalia[1]	1969	7.2
Thailand	1969	16.3
Tunisia[1]	1968	25.2
Uganda	1969	19.4
Finland	1969	23.9
United States[2]	1968	16.6

[1] Ministry of Education only. [2] Provisional.
Source : Unesco: *Statistical yearbook, 1971* (Paris, 1972).

of children, inevitably impoverishes the working population and inhibits employment-creating investment. It is not a question of children being unwanted or unloved: the more they are loved, the more the community spends on them. The welfare and employment aspects of this situation are discussed in later chapters. In the meantime, however, table 2 gives some examples of the expenditure of certain countries on education in the 1960s, as a percentage the government's total expenditure. It is hardly necessary to point out that the poorer the country, the heavier the burden that these percentages represent, nor that they conceal enormous differences in actual expenditure between the "have" and the "have-not" nations. In 1968 the total world outlay by governments on education was approximately the equivalent of $132,000 million, of which less than one-tenth ($12,000 million) was spent in the Third World. At that time the population aged 5 to 24 in the developing countries was about 1,100 million, and in the more developed regions about 350 million. If that age span is taken to represent the potential years of education, it can thus be simply calculated that in 1968 the richer countries spent an average of $380 per young person on education, while the poorer countries averaged less than $11. It is true that developing countries, precisely because of rapid population growth, concentrate educational spending on younger children, so that a somewhat more favourable comparison would emerge if it were based on expenditure at a lower age; but it could not possibly alter the general contrast. Moreover, the population aged 5 to 24 in the developing countries is at present growing by about

30 per cent every decade, compared with about 10 per cent in the more developed regions. Hence the poorer countries would have to expand their present educational expenditure three times as fast as would the richer countries, merely to prevent themselves falling even farther behind.

It is now generally accepted that an educational system, particularly in the developing countries, should reflect much more closely the emerging shape of social and economic development. This involves the educational planner in the complex task of matching the present with the future, and the future with the more distant future, so that, ideally, when his pupils leave school or college they will have the skills and knowledge wanted at that time by their nation, either for immediate employment or for training to higher levels. This is a difficult enough operation in a stable community expanding relatively slowly and enjoying full or nearly full employment. In a developing country characterised by rapid population growth and by mass unemployment —with unemployment heaviest of all among youth—it is, however, virtually impossible.

THE TRAINING LOAD

6

United Nations projections show that during the 1965-75 decade approximately 570 million children in the developing world will pass their fifteenth birthday; during the following decade, 1975-85, approximately 710 million will pass that birthday, and in the 1985-95 decade the number will be about 900 million. These figures give an impression of the rate at which population growth is stacking up what might be called the "crude training load" in the Third World.

If one relates the training load broadly to productive capacity, by taking the ratio between persons aged 15 to 19 and the rest of the population of working age (that is, aged 20 to 64), one finds that in 1970 this ratio was 16 per 100 in the more developed and 22 per 100 in the less developed regions. In Africa it was 23 per 100, in Latin America and the Caribbean 24 per 100, and in southern Asia 20 per 100. In North America it was 18 per 100 and in Europe 12 per 100. In other words, if everybody entitled to training had been receiving it, 100 workers in the developing world would have had to carry 6 more trainees than would 100 workers in the richer countries. The burden on workers in Latin America would have been double the burden on workers in Europe. These figures reflect in part the longer life span of persons in the richer countries, but they are mainly a consequence of differences in fertility rates.

When one considers that the real cost of training a worker, in terms of personnel and material, does not vary greatly from one country to another, the burden on the productive capacity of the poorer, high-fertility countries is seen to be heavier still. If, again, the load could be limited to vocational training in the strict sense, excluding conventional education, the balance of advantage would swing even further away from the developing regions. This is because in the richer countries a far higher proportion of children remain at school after the age of 15.

Population and labour

Table 3. Population aged 15 to 19 years on different fertility assumptions (millions)

Country	Total population in 1965 [1]	Year	High fertility assumption	Low fertility assumption
Colombia	18.02	1965	1.80	1.80
		1985	3.97	3.70
		1990	4.70	4.05
		2000	7.01	4.77
Congo	0.84	1965	0.09	0.09
		1985	0.14	0.13
		1990	0.17	0.15
		2000	0.25	0.20
Costa Rica	1.49	1965	0.15	0.15
		1985	0.34	0.33
		1990	0.43	0.40
		2000	0.64	0.54
Egypt	29.50	1965	3.01	3.01
		1985	5.52	5.34
		1990	6.58	6.14
		2000	9.12	7.20
Ghana	7.74	1965	0.76	0.76
		1985	1.57	1.49
		1990	1.91	1.79
		2000	2.91	2.40
Kenya	9.37	1965	0.98	0.98
		1985	1.90	1.85
		1990	2.37	2.23
		2000	3.48	2.93
Mexico	42.69	1965	4.33	4.33
		1985	9.08	8.85
		1990	10.98	10.23
		2000	15.93	13.86
Nigeria	48.68	1965	5.07	5.07
		1985	8.71	8.26
		1990	10.59	9.62
		2000	15.70	12.71
Senegal	3.49	1965	0.36	0.36
		1985	0.61	0.57
		1990	0.73	0.65
		2000	1.04	0.86
Tunisia	4.36	1965	0.44	0.44
		1985	0.87	0.85
		1990	1.06	1.00
		2000	1.55	1.24
Zaire	15.63	1965	1.58	1.58
		1985	2.59	2.47
		1990	3.17	2.90
		2000	4.59	3.91

[1] i.e. the year in which the assumed decline in fertility begins.
Source: United Nations low and high fertility assumptions (see Chapter 1).

All the figures given so far in this chapter are based on the United Nations Population Division's medium fertility assumption, explained in Chapter 1. The longer-term effects of possible changes in birth rates are brought out very clearly in some projections based on higher and lower fertility assumptions (see table 3). To take Kenya as an example, it will be noted that on the basis of a total population in 1965 (when the projection is launched) of about 9.37 million, there would be an estimated 3.48 million persons aged 15 to 19 to provide for at the end of the century on the higher fertility assumption, compared with fewer than 3 million if fertility rates were reduced to the lower level. In other words, a feasible reduction in fertility (which would still leave birth rates much higher than in most industrial countries) could make a difference of more than 500,000 to the number of persons in the training cohort. By that time the total population of Kenya will be about 25 million, if present trends continue.

This reduction is all the more striking if one remembers that fertility changes cannot have any appreciable effect on the size of the population aged more than a few months until several years have elapsed. A glance at table 3 will, in fact, show that there is practically no difference between the lower and higher forecasts of the 15 to 19 age-group in any of the countries until some time between 1985 and 1990, or 20 to 25 years after the starting point. Beyond the turn of the century, the gap would widen dramatically.

In the most populous country listed, Nigeria, which in 1965 had a total population approaching 49 million, the difference in the number of persons aged 15 to 19 at the end of the century on the two fertility assumptions is 3 million. In the least populous, Congo, it is about 50,000. One can only conjecture what results would have been obtained if similar calculations had been made for the whole of the developing world, including countries like India (with a population in 1965 approaching 500 million) or China (with a 1965 population exceeding 700 million).

CHILD WORKERS: A SPECIAL PROBLEM

One of the first effects of rapid population growth can be seen in the large numbers of children and adolescents who have dropped out of school, who never went to school, or who have not enrolled for intermediate school at the age of 12. Many of these children attempt to obtain employment, or are put to work by their elders, with little or no training worth the name. Several estimates have been made of the extent of child labour. The lowest of these surmises that at least 43 million children aged 14 or under were "economically active" in 1970. Of this total, more than 41 million were in the Third World and 2 million were in the less advanced of the so-called advanced nations. If one may assume that the infant labourers were *at least* 5 years old, then in 1970, 1 out of every 16 Third World children aged between 5 and 14 was a worker. Thankfully, this is one number that is not increasing; in fact, according to this estimate the world total appears to have fallen by about 2 million in the decade 1960-70. Even so, these figures are, as we have said, the lowest of the various estimates, and the ILO's *Labour force projections 1965-1985*, for instance, puts the 1970 total at 54 million, only 3 million fewer than the figure 20 years earlier.

FACILITIES ALREADY INADEQUATE

In many countries workers' training facilities already fall short of the anticipated demand, even on the basis of economic planning related to production targets rather than to employment creation. In Latin America, for example, it has been estimated that an additional 13 million skilled operatives and artisans will be required between 1965 and 1980, plus nearly 32 million semi-skilled workers. On the (surely optimistic) assumptions that the semi-skilled workers would require no organised training and that students educated in secondary technical schools could adapt to skilled employment also without further instruction, a shortfall of 7 million persons would remain to be trained in vocational training institutions after leaving school. On the whole, Latin American countries have made impressive advances in vocational training in recent years, but this load would still exceed current capacity.

In the First Malaysia Plan (1966-70) it was estimated that total requirements of skilled workers in Malaysia would be more than 32,000 during the Plan period, while the anticipated output was only 23,000. The Second Five-Year Plan of Thailand (1966-71) anticipated a deficit of about 10,000 trained craftsmen. The Lebanese Department of Labour estimated that 4,600 additional technicians were required in Lebanon annually, while the output from technical training establishments in 1970 was about 400 and was expected to be not more than 600 in 1971.

If full employment is assumed, the implied training load is very much heavier. A report on human resources and education prepared by the Peruvian National Planning Institute in collaboration with the Organisation for Economic Co-operation and Development, published in 1966, contains some telling estimates of the soaring demand for trained personnel in a medium-sized country whose population is growing at 3 per cent per annum. In 1971 the population of Peru was about 14 million. The report shows that the labour force, which was 3.1 million in 1961, is expected to reach 5.8 million in 1980, an increase approaching 90 per cent. Moreover, by that date it is anticipated that only 2.1 million of the 1961 labour force will still be at work, leaving 3.7 million new entrants for whom some sort of training will have been required in the intervening 19 years. The estimated demand for technicians in 1980 is put at 146,000, of whom all but 15,400 will be newcomers: a sixfold expansion. The demand for skilled workers is expected to be nearly four times greater, rising from just over 91,000 in 1961 to 351,000 in 1980. Of this total, about 62,000 will remain of the 1961 workforce, leaving a training load of 289,000. These estimates are in addition to those for professional and managerial staff and for the big corps of semi-skilled workers; for both of these groups also, substantial increases are projected.

The Peruvian report was not a plan for full employment but an attempt to assess the education and training needs of the country on reasonable assumptions of how different sectors of the labour force might be expected to expand as the population grows. If a similar exercise were carried out for other developing countries with rapidly expanding populations, the findings, in principle, would doubtless be much the same. A major assumption of the report was that the economy, developing in the way anticipated, would absorb the 2.7 million additional workers. The soundness of this assumption can only be tested by time. It does not affect the general validity of the estimated training load, unless such estimates are to be related to expectations of failure and mass unemployment.

TRAINING FOR FULL EMPLOYMENT

The training effort called for by a positive policy for full employment was already revealed very forcibly in the first two major country reports prepared by ILO missions under the World Employment Programme, those for Colombia and Sri Lanka. The Colombia proposals call for the creation of 5 million new jobs between 1970 and 1985, of which no fewer than 4 million will be required simply to keep pace with the growth of the labour force, now swelling by 3.5 per cent every year. The report says: "The employment strategy proposed in this report has important implications in terms of both the volume and the direction of required vocational training. Not only would the much higher growth rate required in the various sectors involve large numbers of trained workers, but the crucial role of rural development and the expansion of craft and small-scale manufacturing in the framework of the over-all strategy would call for sizeable increases in personnel with qualifications that in the past have received relatively little emphasis."

In Sri Lanka the labour force, which was 4.1 million in 1968, is expected to reach 5.2 million in 1976, an increase of more than 25 per cent in eight years. For the years following 1976 estimates have been made by the Ministry of Planning and Employment on three different fertility assumptions. All three naturally yield a similar figure (6.3 million) for 1985, when the labour force will still consist of persons already born. By 1998, however, the probabilities diverge, from a low estimate of 8.31 million to a high of 9.34 million. Thus we may say that between 1968 and 1985 the labour force will almost certainly grow by more than 50 per cent, and that in the 13 years following it could grow by another 30 per cent if fertility rates are at the higher level, or by about 25 per cent if fertility is lower. The possible reduction in fertility makes a difference of 1 million in the number of workers who will have to be trained, one way or another, for employment over the 13-year period.

The mission to Sri Lanka aimed at full employment (defined as 95 per cent of the labour force gainfully occupied) by 1985. Allowing for existing unemployment, this would entail creating 2.8 million more jobs than existed in 1968. (These figures are discussed more fully in the chapters dealing with employment.) And of those new jobs to be created, at least 2.1 million would be required simply to offset population growth.

This enormous undertaking will have repercussions not only on the numbers of workers to be trained but also on the skills in which they should be instructed. The mission to Sri Lanka, like that to Colombia, emphasised the importance of alternative production techniques: "Choice of technology is a key instrument in an employment strategy for Ceylon.[1] How Ceylon chooses to produce various commodities and services will vitally affect employment opportunities and income distribution. [. . .] Thus, the authorities will have to determine how best to allocate scarce resources in labour-intensive but *efficient* techniques of production."

The mission underscores the point with a striking illustration, drawn from a study by C. Dharmawardana entitled *Manpower versus machines*, published by Vidyodaya University. In this study Dharmawardana compared the actual costs of building the Dambara-Thimbirana road with an estimate of the probable costs if more human labour instead of machine power had been employed. The human labour wins by 7.4 Rupees (about $1) per cubic foot as against 27 Rupees; the time taken, 125 days, is the same. That is not all. One technique used 6 machines and 14 men; the other would employ no machines and 136 men. The ILO mission points out that there could be some exaggeration in this estimate, as the effect on the workers' health and physique should not be overlooked. Even if an intermediate technique were selected, however, the lesson for vocational training is the same. To train or not to train: a small élite of highly sophisticated machine operators, or a larger number of men using manual skills?

The possibilities of alternative production techniques are bound to receive increasing attention, as governments re-think their development policies

---

[1] The name by which Sri Lanka was known at the time of the mission.

in terms of employment needs. It is as much a question of which economic activities should be encouraged, where there is a choice, as of the techniques to be employed on a given task. This reappraisal now seems certain to be accelerated by the World Employment Programme.

Linked with this question as to which occupations should be encouraged is the problem of rural-urban migration, much of it the result of population pressure on the land. Everybody agrees that the retreat from the land should at least be retarded—few believe it can be stopped, at all events in the foreseeable future. There is also general agreement that the exodus cannot be moderated without an extensive rural development programme entailing a big advance in rural skills.

Let us, then, first look at the training picture in the countryside, and then in the towns.

TRAINING FOR RURAL DEVELOPMENT

7

The exodus from the land is not confined to countries with high rates of population growth. On the contrary, it still persists to such a degree in low fertility countries that it can be calculated that something like one villager in two may be expected to quit the land in the richer parts of the world before the turn of the century, and that for every ten townsmen now living in such countries another six will be added, two of them having drifted in from the land. When one considers that twice as many people already live in the towns in these countries as live in the countryside, this estimated migration is all the more remarkable. Why, then, put so much stress on rural migration as a special problem of population growth in the developing countries?

The short answer appears to be that excessive population growth accentuates the situation so much that the problem takes on different proportions. The total population of the developing world is expected to double in the 30-year period between 1970 and the turn of the century, from approximately 2,500 million to some 5,000 million. Of this estimated growth, about 1,000 million will still be in rural areas and 1,500 million in the towns (see table 4 and figure 8). If these projections are borne out, the rural population will fall to well short of 60 per cent of the whole: but nevertheless there will still be upwards of 700 million more persons to care for in the villages of Asia, upwards of 30 million more in those of Latin America and some 230 million more in African villages than there were in 1970.

Notwithstanding this residual growth, it can be argued that migration mainly creates problems for the towns. It certainly places a heavy extra burden on towns, approximately doubling the average rate at which they would otherwise be growing in the developing world. The towns, however, can do little to turn back this tide. Hence action is required in the countryside if only to mitigate the consequences in the cities, and this in turn places a heavy burden on the tenuous development resources of the village, including

Figure 8.   Urban and rural populations of the less developed regions, 1950-2000

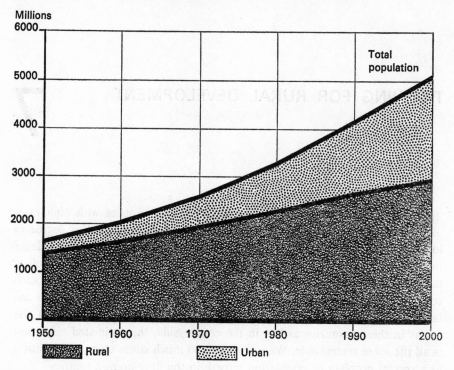

Source: United Nations Population Division.

its educational resources and its meagre vocational training facilities for young people. Furthermore, as we have seen, the rural exodus is proceeding very much faster in the Third World than in the developed regions. The reasons are complex, but there can be no doubt that a considerable part of the younger generation's disenchantment with the rural prospect in developing countries can be attributed in part to the consequences of population pressure on the land.

The rural exodus may appear to ease the employment problem in the countryside—that will be discussed later—but it does not necessarily reduce the training load. As we shall see in the next chapter, few of the migrants obtain any worthwhile training when they reach the towns; hence such training as they may receive in their lives will have been provided during their early years in the village. The extent to which the national authorities contribute to the cost of this training from taxes collected from the nation as a whole will vary from country to country. It is certain that a good part of the load, at least, falls on the rural community which, poor enough to

Table 4. Urban and rural population (millions)

Region	Urban population	Rural population	Total population	Percentage of urban to total population
World				
1950	*704*	*1 782*	*2 486*	*28.32*
1960	*985*	*1 997*	*2 982*	*33.04*
1970	*1 352*	*2 280*	*3 632*	*37.19*
1980	*1 854*	*2 614*	*4 467*	*41.50*
1990	*2 517*	*2 939*	*5 456*	*46.14*
2000	*3 329*	*3 186*	*6 515*	*51.10*
More developed regions				
1950	439	418	858	51.22
1960	582	394	976	59.63
1970	717	374	1 091	65.74
1980	864	347	1 210	71.36
1990	1 021	316	1 337	76.39
2000	1 174	280	1 454	80.74
Less developed regions				
1950	265	1 363	1 628	16.26
1960	403	1 603	2 005	20.09
1970	632	1 910	2 542	24.96
1980	990	2 267	3 257	30.40
1990	1 496	2 623	4 120	36.33
2000	2 155	2 906	5 061	42.59
Eastern Asia				
1950	105	552	657	15.93
1960	179	601	780	22.90
1970	266	664	930	28.63
1980	387	708	1 095	35.35
1990	541	725	1 265	42.73
2000	722	703	1 424	50.67
Southern Asia				
1950	111	587	698	15.91
1960	154	711	865	17.82
1970	238	888	1 126	21.15
1980	370	1 116	1 486	24.91
1990	556	1 355	1 912	29.11
2000	793	1 561	2 354	33.69
Africa				
1950	30	187	217	14.02
1960	48	221	270	17.93
1970	77	268	344	22.24
1980	125	332	457	27.30
1990	203	413	616	32.97
2000	320	498	818	39.15
Latin America				
1950	66	97	162	40.47
1960	103	110	213	48.35
1970	158	125	283	55.89
1980	238	139	377	63.23
1990	350	150	500	69.98
2000	495	157	652	75.93

NB: the figures may not add up to the totals shown owing to rounding.
Source : United Nations Population Division.

begin with, receives no return on the investment. In fact, in many developing countries it can be shown that taxes on farm incomes, or indirectly on farm produce, have been used to subsidise industrial development in the towns.

THE WORST OF BOTH WORLDS

If education alone is considered, the facts speak for themselves. Nearly all the migrants to the towns have already completed whatever schooling they are to have. This may be a not inconsiderable amount, because generally it is precisely the young people who have had some education who decide to quit the land. Figures gathered by a joint ILO/UNICEF mission in the Ivory Coast in 1968 showed that in some rural areas 97 per cent of children who obtained the primary school leaving certificate migrated eventually to the towns, while 90 per cent of those who never went to school remained in the village. A survey of former pupils from 77 village schools in four main regions of the country revealed that only 25 per cent of the final-year pupils of 1966/67 were still living in the village in October 1968. Some of the pupils had gone on to secondary schools in larger centres, but they were assumed to be lost to the land; and of the 25 per cent who remained in the village only a year after the end of the school period many would no doubt emigrate within a few more years. A study of young people born in the village who were in the 15 to 24 age-group in 1967 showed that 61 per cent of the males and 75 per cent of the females with primary school certificates had already moved to the towns. Of all who could read and write, 42 per cent of the males and 55 per cent of the females aged 15 to 24 had left, but of the total illiterates 92 per cent of the males and 89 per cent of the females remained in the village. Thus the migratory exodus drains away from the countryside its most promising young people.

THE VIEWPOINT OF YOUTH

A young person may not even begin to understand the relationship between employment and the supply of capital in the city, but he can see with his own eyes the relationship between employment and the supply of land round his native village. This is strikingly confirmed in a paper by John Anderson which appeared in *Teacher Education* (Oxford) in February 1968. In two case studies of young people in different rural areas in the Central Province of Kenya, where school attendance was virtually 100 per cent, Anderson first put a questionnaire to 252 boys and 176 girls, mostly aged 13 to 16, who were in the last year of primary school in a village about 100 miles from Nairobi. One of the objects was to discover what sort of job the young people hoped eventually to obtain. Of these 252 country boys, the total number wishing to work directly in farming was 26, or almost exactly 10 per cent, although almost all the boys must have come from farming families. Some of those who wanted to become teachers could no doubt be added to the rural options. Of the 176 girls, only five plumped for farming.

In the second case study 203 boys were traced who two years before had been in the last class of a primary school in a fairly prosperous, well populated market-gardening area about 15 miles from the capital. It was found that 41.5 per cent had gone on to secondary school, 15.5 per cent had returned to primary school with the intention of passing their examinations at a second attempt, 9 per cent were in wage employment (the majority of whom—12 out of 18—had left home), 2 per cent had left the village but could not be reached, and the remaining 32 per cent, or 65 in all, were unemployed, in the sense that they did not have a regular paid occupation. In fact, these 65 represented more than three-quarters of the total number of boys who were not still at school and who could be traced. In any case they made up one-third of the entire class, and it was expected that they would be joined in due course by many of the 32 boys who had returned to the primary school for another shot at the examination.

Some of the boys had been to the towns in search of employment, but had returned empty-handed, having after all no modern skills to offer. Nearly all of them worked (and in some cases worked hard) when needed on the family farm, but not one of them saw this as his future life, nor apparently did their parents. Asked to state their aspirations, 10 still hankered after a place in a secondary school, 33 wanted a job in a factory—presumably in a town—and only four would have welcomed a patch of ground in a land settlement scheme. (This was at the time when a million acres of the former "White Highlands" were being redistributed among African farmers.) Since few of the boys who had gone on to secondary school were likely to be dreaming of a plot of land in a resettlement scheme, it is quite possible that these four were the only members of the original 203 schoolboys who saw this as their way of life.

One of the reasons why none of them had a future on the family farm may be inferred from the fact that most of them had at least three brothers. The farm, small enough already as a general rule, would have to be divided into four on their father's death. Before his death, assuming that the sons married, it would have to support five families where formerly it supported one.

TRAINING AND LAND REFORM

Many of the boys in the first case study evidently saw the possibilities of modern farming, *provided* that land was available and that they could be trained in the required skills. Training and land reform, indeed, are two of the keys to rural development, for where population pressure has led to a demand for new farmland, either by the breaking-up of big estates or the opening-up of virgin land by irrigation and clearance schemes, the operation can be wrecked if it is not accompanied by an appropriate training programme.

The speed at which land reform can be carried out may well depend on the rate at which such programmes can supply trained personnel. The ILO Colombia mission estimated that, even allowing for an exodus to the towns of approximately half of the young people entering the rural labour force between 1970 and 1985, the rural economy would still have to support some 800,000 extra workers, let alone their families, at the end of the 15-year period. The agricultural labour force being about 2.5 million in 1970, this would mean four people living off the land or in village employment in 1985 for every three in 1970. After making an optimistic estimate of the numbers who might obtain wage employment in a more flourishing rural community, the mission concluded that 25,000 workers would have to be provided with new land *every year*, "merely to preserve the present unsatisfactory status quo".

The Colombia mission agreed that land settlement at the rate it proposed might outrun the provision of supporting services, but it was so concerned with population pressure that it felt the risk should be taken: "To have peasants enjoy low income with at least subsistence is probably better than their joining the swelling ranks of the unemployed in the towns." In other words, if the pace of land reform required by population growth were achieved, it might very easily create a training load in the rural areas that could not be carried in the short run, but this possibility would have to be faced for demographic reasons.

SHORTAGE OF TRAINED MANPOWER

There is widespread agreement on the need for a big expansion of rural training facilities if the land is to support a growing population. The mission to Sri Lanka remarked, in an appendix on training: "One of the most striking features of the agricultural sector is shortage of trained manpower, a feature which is something of a paradox in a predominantly agricultural economy characterised by an increasing number of educated unemployed." UNIDO manpower forecasts for Latin America assume an increase in skilled agricultural workers in that region from 1.7 million in 1965 to 4.9 million in 1980, and of semi-skilled landworkers from 5.2 million to 14.8 million—that is, approximately a threefold expansion of both groups. During the same period the numbers of unskilled agricultural workers would remain virtually unchanged at about 28 million. In fact, unskilled labourers, who in 1965 constituted 80 per cent of the agricultural labour force, were expected to comprise only 60 per cent (of a much bigger labour force) 15 years later. The total number of workers employed in agriculture was expected to grow in the 15 years from less than 35 million to more than 48 million.

Obviously, a much improved standard of living would be required to keep so many extra workers on the land in Latin America. With millions still expected to work as unskilled hands, the rural prospect cannot seem too bright for young people who have been to school. Their disillusionment is anticipated in the projections for employment outside agriculture, which is expected to double in the 15 years while the agricultural workforce is growing by about a third.

An ILO seminar on the organisation of vocational training in Arab States observed in its report: "An overwhelming proportion of young people in Arab countries is growing up without the benefit of any organised vocational and technical education or training. Important sectors of the economy are not served at all by the systems of vocational and technical education and training. In consequence, these sectors are not provided with the technical leadership required for their modernisation." In Africa, where there is still much virgin land, a major constraint on development in many areas is the primitive technology used for breaking and cultivating the soil. The land could support bigger populations at higher standards if farmers were trained in more modern techniques calling for only slightly more sophisticated capital equipment.

If the population challenge is to be met, rural workers will have to be trained in increasing numbers for a wide range of skills. Besides the sizeable workforce required for the public service alone (for building roads and railways, improving river transport, combating floods and erosion, and so on), thousands of skilled craftsmen will be needed to produce basic consumer goods, to service the farms and to man the new rural industries. If the land is to support a rapidly increasing population, the village community needs to benefit far more than it does today, in many areas, from its economic potential. To achieve this entails not simply expanding the output from the soil and from animal husbandry and fisheries, but also carrying the processing of rural products up to a much more advanced point on the economic chain. At present a countryman may sell hides to an agent (probably a town dweller) who trucks the hides to a town, where all the subsequent operations are carried out—tanning, processing, dyeing, making up into leatherware and, finally, selling to an exporter or to the consumer. In some cases the hide may even be sent to a different country at the other end of the world, where the value added at each stage does not even accrue to the producer nation, let alone the villager. With the aid of farmers' co-operatives, much of this development can be kept in the village, even to the operation of the motor transport to the town or at least to the railway station. The immense and varied training effort that this implies can be imagined. Not least important is the need for training officials to manage the co-operative societies.

A MAJOR CONSTRAINT

One of the heaviest drags on rural development is the shortage of agricultural extension workers, the men and women who make periodic visits to farmers, bringing advice and guidance. Even in countries where farmers are generally well educated and have the benefit of the latest equipment and specialist literature, the agricultural extension worker is considered a key factor in the promotion of rural prosperity. Yet an ILO team conducting a pilot rural employment promotion project in western Nigeria found, during a preliminary inquiry conducted in 1966, that 70 per cent of the farmers in the area had never seen an extension worker and only 14 per cent had seen one during the previous six months. This is not surprising when one learns that there were six general extension workers for 27,000 to 28,000 farms. The Colombia mission also found that the shortage of agricultural extension workers was a major constraint on rural promotion, although the situation there, as one would expect, was more promising than in rural Africa. None the less: "The training of intermediate technicians has long been one of the worst problems hampering agricultural progress in Colombia. [. . .] Such technicians provide a source for the recruitment of all types of experts in direct contact with the agricultural workers, such as extension workers. An extremely high demand is anticipated in the next few years, the numbers needed running into thousands." In this case the United Nations Development Programme was stepping into the breach with a Unesco project for agricultural training institutes with a planned output of 4,000 technicians a year.

The United Nations Economic Commission for Latin America estimated that for Latin America as a whole the numbers of professional and technical workers in agriculture should be raised from about 40,000 in 1965 to 200,000 in 1980, quite apart from the urgent need to improve the skills of farmers. The ILO mission to Sri Lanka observed, in the appendix on training mentioned above: "A general gap observed in Ceylon's manpower training programme is the dearth of farm management specialists to guide and supervise village workers' activities and also to involve themselves directly in extension work by acting as a bridge between the village workers and the subject-matter specialists. This middle tier in the extension programme is conspicuous by its absence. [. . .] Our proposals envisage a huge rural works programme. For the success of this programme it is vital to have a large number of trained overseers and other staff of similar level who can assist in the engineering aspect of the rural works programme under the guidance of the trained engineers. There are three categories of people on whose performance the success of our scheme largely hinges: co-operative managers, farm management specialists and overseers. If the programme is to succeed, these categories of people will be needed in thousands. Those in charge of planning manpower and training will need to estimate the scale and pattern of requirements. . . ." The development programme of Madagascar stresses that the total number of technical and professional agricultural staff should double every five years. The Indian Fourth Five-Year Plan (1969-74) provides for the establishment of four new agricultural universities, in addition to the nine already in existence.

BACKLOG OF NEGLECT

Rural illiteracy remains a serious problem in most parts of the developing world. As we noted in Chapter 5, school facilities in both town and country have difficulty in keeping up with population growth, but the problem is more acute in the countryside with its long backlog of neglect. The drop-out rate, too, is higher in the country. If to this is added the fact that illiterates tend to remain in the village while educated youth migrates to the towns, the gravity of the problem can be imagined. An illiterate farmer is not necessarily unskilled or unintelligent, but there is a limit to the further training from which he might benefit, especially when it embodies technical and mechanical concepts that can only be conveyed by figures and diagrams. When he makes the breakthrough into cash farming he may be at a disadvantage if he can make only the simplest commercial calculations. Indeed, he is often handicapped even before he has planted his crop. In a rice-growing province of Iran agricultural experts explained to farmers that they should use 34 kilograms of seed to 1 hectare of land. It was later found that few of the peasants knew enough arithmetic to apply this ratio to their holdings. As a consequence they were using 14,000 tons too much seed every year, at an unnecessary cost equal to $2.8 million. This was the position when Unesco was approached to start a "work-oriented" literacy project—that is, a programme combining literacy teaching with vocational training.

An ILO rural development expert was confronted with a similar difficulty in Senegal, where groundnut farmers had been told that for best results 150 kilograms of fertiliser should be spread over 1 hectare of land. He overcame it by advising Senegalese extension workers to teach farmers how to measure 100 square metres (that is, one-hundredth of a hectare) at a time by pacing out a square 10 metres wide. On this surface they spread 1.5 kilograms of fertiliser from a basket containing just that amount. This neatly solved the problem—one problem—but it indicates how far the world still has to go in raising the skills and knowledge of its farmworkers if the land is to support an increasing population at a standard of comfort worthy of human beings. Nearly all developing countries are making tremendous efforts in this direction, but every day the load gets heavier. No wonder millions of young people are turning their backs on village life.

TRAINING AND INDUSTRY 8

The paradox of rural-urban migration at the rate it has now reached in most developing countries is that neither community seems to benefit. The village, having sustained the emigrant through his years of childhood dependency, loses him when he has reached the age at which he might be contributing to the common good. The town, with its capital resources and its capacity for orderly growth stretched to the limit by its own town-born youth, takes in yet another bright-eyed youngster from the fields, to whom it cannot offer employment or even a roof. If he hopes to enrol for further education or vocational training, he finds that the streets are teeming with young people of his own generation, many of them better equipped for city life because they were born there, others like himself newcomers to the pavements.

In Africa, Kinshasa, the capital of Zaire, actually doubled its population in the five years between 1945 and 1950 (a growth rate approaching 20 per cent per annum), doubled it again in the ten years following, and then doubled it in the seven years to 1967. That is to say, between 1945 and 1967—less than a generation—the population of this African metropolis grew nearly nine times. As for the future, the Zairian Deputy Minister for Labour and Social Affairs has given an estimated population for Kinshasa of 1.7 million for the year 1977, and explained that, according to Zaire's principal statistical sources, under the combined effect of natural growth and migration the doubling of the population in a little under ten years was the hypothesis to follow. If natural growth alone were multiplying the city's inhabitants, the population of Kinshasa would be growing at about the same rate as that of Zaire as a whole: it would be doubling approximately every 30 years. And that growth rate, as we have already noted, would in itself be creating enough problems for vocational training authorities.

In 1967 the average age of the population of Kinshasa was 17 years and 10 months; 62 per cent of the population were under 20 years of age, and

70 per cent under 25. Some 460,000 out of the 865,000 people living in the city were immigrants, and newcomers were coming in at a rate of 800 a week. Kinshasa is not exceptional. In Africa as a whole, the number of rural immigrants in a town's population is seldom less than 50 per cent and in some towns it is 90 per cent.

The picture in Asia is much the same. The Calcutta metropolitan area at the 1961 census had 6.6 million inhabitants, of whom 3.1 million had been born there and 3.5 million were migrants. At the 1941 census the Calcutta-born population of the metropolitan area had exceeded the migrant population, but by 1961 these locally born people were outnumbered by the newcomers. In recent years the major cities of other Asian countries have in most cases grown more rapidly than have Indian cities. Between 1950 and 1970, Peking grew four times; Karachi, Lahore, Djakarta and Bandung, three times; Manila and Bangkok, two-and-a-half times. During the same period Calcutta and Bombay increased their populations by about one-half, yet the continuance of even this relatively low rate of population growth places the civic resources under a barely tolerable strain. The Indian Fourth Five-Year Plan (1969-74), in its section on urban development, observed that the situation in regard to growth of population in metropolitan centres, particularly of Calcutta and Bombay, was already so difficult as to make it almost a law-and-order problem, and that, to a lesser extent, this was also true of several other large cities. The chances of the newcomer from the fields or from a small town entering a vocational training establishment to be prepared for a useful career in the city are, in these circumstances, obviously minimal.

That the spiralling rate of urban growth, however caused, is a world-wide phenomenon is clear from figure 9. In most of the major cities of Latin America the migrant inflow equals, if it does not exceed, the city's natural growth; the ILO Colombia mission noted that the country's four largest cities, not just the capital, were growing at 7 per cent per annum, or much more than double the rate for the nation as a whole. Bogotá itself grew four times between 1950 and 1970, and if this pace is maintained the city's population could well top 7 million by 1985. During the same two decades, Guadalajara and Caracas grew more than three times; Rio de Janeiro, Lima and Montevideo grew two-and-a-half times, and Santiago doubled its population. Buenos Aires almost doubled and Mexico City grew by about a half.

Often the migrant moves first from his village to a small town, while others are moving from the small towns to larger ones and from the larger towns to the cities. Thus the basic figures for rural-urban migration, reflecting simply the numbers who have left the land, tend to conceal much of the movement into the big cities, which might be classified as inter-urban. Just

Figure 9. Growth of cities, 1950, 1960, 1970

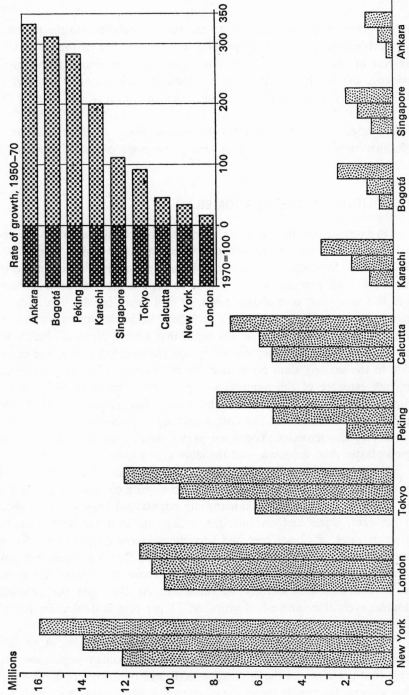

Source : United Nations: *Housing, building and planning: problems and priorities in human settlements*, Report of the Secretary-General to the General Assembly on item 49 of the provisional agenda, 25th Session, 1970 (New York, doc. A/8037).

as the urban is growing faster than the rural population, so the population of the big cities is frequently growing faster than that of the small towns. Several of the Asian and Latin American cities mentioned above provide evidence of this trend. A survey in Santiago, for example, revealed that 42 per cent of all migrants came from other urban areas, and one for Delhi showed that 65 per cent of migrants had "graduated" to the capital, so to speak, after living in several smaller towns. Some of them had sampled 15 other towns before moving to Delhi, and none of the 65 per cent had tried fewer than six.

THE PLIGHT OF THE NEWCOMER

On average, therefore, the influx from the countryside accounts for about half the growth rate of the urban population in the Third World. Where do all these hundreds of thousands of former country dwellers make their home? For all practical purposes it is so certain that the rural immigrant will live in a slum or a shanty town, or will camp in what the authorities call an "uncontrolled settlement", or indeed lie in the streets without even a piece of cardboard to cover his head, that United Nations officials work on the assumption that they can safely add the total influx from the country-side to the existing slum population for the purpose of making an accurate enough estimate of the numbers living in these "crowded, filthy and dis-ruptive" conditions. The result of this endless flow of migrants to the slums and shanty towns is that the fastest-growing communities in the world are these very communities. The town grows faster than the village, the city grows faster than the town, and the slum grows faster than the city.

A report submitted to the United Nations General Assembly in 1970 put it succinctly: "While population in developing countries typically grows at 2 to 3 per cent annually and many city populations grow at rates exceeding 6 per cent, slums and uncontrolled settlements in urban areas commonly grow at rates of 12 per cent and sometimes exceed 20 per cent." Some of the problems created by communities growing at 2 to 3 per cent per annum were briefly indicated in an earlier chapter. Those of a community growing at 20 per cent can scarcely be imagined. At that rate the population doubles every three-and-a-half years. At 12 per cent it doubles in less than six years.

The slum population of Nairobi is reported to be growing at an annual rate of 25 to 30 per cent, while the total metropolitan population grows by 6 to 8 per cent and the population of Kenya by 3.3 per cent. This means that whereas the population of the country as a whole doubles every 21 years, the population of the metropolis doubles every 10 years and the population of the city's slums doubles in less than three years. Between 1950 and 1960 the slum population of Rio de Janeiro at least doubled (and according to some estimates increased four to five times), while the non-slum population of the city grew by only one-third. The 1961 census of Calcutta revealed that at least 2.2 million people, one-third of the total population, lived in slums and uncontrolled settlements: 600,000 of them slept in the streets. The squatter population of Manila more than doubled in the six years from 1962 to 1968, during which another 400,000 were added to the total. In Ankara 60 per cent of the population are squatters. So are half the population of Guayaquíl, a city in Ecuador with a population of 750,000 in 1968. The slum and squatter settlements of all Brazilian cities with more than 100,000 inhabitants are expected to multiply six times in the next 12 years. . . .

THE LACK OF OPPORTUNITY

The social consequences of growth rates like these need not detain us at this point. Nor, frankly, need the implications for the training of workers do so for very long. It is enough to observe that this, indeed, is the manner in which the major cities of the Third World are developing. A thimbleful from the sea of young people living in these conditions may be lifted out for vocational training, but for all but a tiny fraction the door of opportunity is firmly shut. A few of the children may be chosen for vocational preparation centres, but the weight of the problem pressing on the urban authorities is practically insupportable. It is normally out of the question to provide special training facilities for the migrants from the countryside who, as we have seen, comprise the great bulk of the squatters and the slum inhabitants. Their numbers are simply growing too fast for anything to be organised for them on the required scale, or, generally, on any scale at all. To discuss the training of young people in the urban centres of the developing world, without first acknowledging that fact, would be to disregard the core of the problem.

Thus for most of the children and adolescents of these slums and squatter settlements there is no way out. Many of the small children flock into the city each day, to work as shoeblacks or newspaper vendors. These are the "wealthy" ones with a morsel of capital. Others offer to wash your car, sing and dance for a few coppers in cafés, or simply beg in the streets. At night they come back to the shanty town, veritable commuters. The number of children leading this life is not even known. In some cities they move about in bands, orphaned or outcast, depending on each other for whatever solace or encouragement the struggle for existence requires. They are what the phrase "rapid population growth" means when it is brought to life. Its influence on training is that these youngsters almost certainly won't get any.

Yet despite the desperate need for qualified manpower in the Third World, industrial training facilities in many developing countries are often under-utilised. Ironically, it is most frequently the poorest countries that waste most resources in this respect. Often there are organisational shortcomings and training programmes are not flexible enough. Sometimes the training is inadequate or too theoretical because of the shortage of qualified instructors, training materials and equipment. Employers may not be aware of the training needs of their workforce, especially where they can easily sell shoddy goods on the market, and they may in any case have little notion of machine maintenance or productivity. There is frequently a discrepancy also between modern training centres and archaic production methods and backward conditions of work in industry, with the result that trained workers cannot employ their newly acquired modern skills. With the youth population growing as never before, these shortcomings will obviously have to be overcome before any sort of equation can be struck between training needs and training opportunities in the developing countries.

Although for many years to come a majority of the workers in these countries will still be in agriculture, the industrialisation programmes already projected still imply a huge expansion of the trained labour force in the towns. Studies made by the United Nations Economic Commission for Africa show that the manpower requirements for industrialisation projects already planned in that continent (not counting the Republic of South Africa) would call for an additional 2 million industrial workers between 1965 and 1975. UNIDO, in the document referred to in the last chapter, estimated the increased needs of Latin America in skilled and semi-skilled workers outside agriculture between 1965 and 1980 at more than 15 million, a rise of more than 160 per cent.

An interesting deduction from the Latin American figures is that the ratio of skilled and semi-skilled workers to unskilled will rise from 3:2 in 1965 to 3:1 in 1980 if the forecasts are borne out. In fact, the estimated increase in unskilled workers outside agriculture over the 15-year period is only of the order of 13 per cent, compared with the 160 per cent increase in the ranks of the skilled and semi-skilled mentioned above. These estimates do not include technicians or professional staffs. During the same period the growth of the labour force as a whole in Latin America is put at approximately 60 per cent. Another way of interpreting the figures would be to say that, out of that 60 per cent, 28 are expected to be in agriculture, 30 to be skilled and semi-skilled workers outside agriculture and only 2 would be unskilled labourers outside agriculture. On these assumptions, even the impressive industrial training facilities now being built up in many Latin American countries will be under heavy pressure.

FINANCIAL IMPLICATIONS

The high cost of training is forcing governments with swelling manpower and limited capital to look very closely at unit training costs. The expense of producing a skilled machine operator for modern industry is particularly high, requiring as it does costly installations for practical work. As José Farré Morán, the managing director of the Spanish occupational upgrading programme, said in the ILO periodical *Training for progress:* "Any country which is making strenuous efforts to achieve industrialisation and economic growth [. . .] is obliged to seek a drastic reduction in the unit cost of training. At the same time it must ensure that the training reaches the greatest possible number of workers. One way of achieving this is to give up all idea of constructing large and impressive training centres, which are expensive both to build and to maintain." Angus Maddison, in a report to UNIDO, observed that in 1967 apprenticeship training was available for only about 3,000 workers in Pakistan, representing not more than 2 or 3 per cent of juveniles in industry. He contrasted this with the 60 per cent of juveniles who obtain apprenticeship training in Brazil, and added that apprenticeship training in firms was less costly and quicker than in schools, and that Pakistan could learn a useful lesson from the Brazilian system.

ANOTHER VICIOUS CIRCLE

This is not the place to pursue this subject. One of the constraints on training within industry is that a well developed industrial sector must exist before apprenticeship training can be provided on a wide scale—another of the vicious circles in which developing countries are caught. No doubt all the recognised forms of training have a place in the developing world. The question is: what combination of methods will best serve a country, an economic sector or an individual industry faced with the need to train a rapidly growing labour force on the slenderest of budgets? A similar question is being asked with increasing persistence about the financing of training, given the ever-mounting claims of education and the welfare services in high fertility societies on the public purse. How much should be borne by the trainee or his family, how much by the State, how much by industry itself? How should industry's share be contributed? By a levy? By a rebate for firms which run a successful apprenticeship scheme? A great deal of study and experience will be required before these questions can be answered with confidence.

In its Plan of Work published in 1969, the Pakistan Manpower Council observed: "Skill requirements must be seen in long-term perspective. The schooling and systematic training of a foreman in industry normally takes

LABOUR-INTENSIVE INDUSTRY – II *(Above)*

SLUMS IN LATIN AMERICA *(Below)*

between 10 and 15 years and the education of a person for a profession normally takes between 15 and 20 years. Because of this long gestation period for skills and because the educational and training system of any country can only be gradually adjusted to the needs of economic growth, there is no meaningful short-term approach to these problems."

With these long periods of gestation, and with the numbers of young workers mounting all the time, developing countries are obviously right to insist that the training system should be related to the national development plan, however gradual the adjustment might have to be in practice. This time-scale makes it all the more important that economic development, planned employment creation and the formulation of training programmes should go hand in hand from the beginning. One must train for employment, obviously, but what sort of employment and how much employment will the future offer? And can education or training—whatever their quantity and quality—solve the economic problems of a rapidly increasing population?

THE EMPLOYMENT GAP

9

Productive employment, as the economic textbooks remind us, is the result of bringing together into useful conjunction the three essential elements in production—natural resources, labour resources and capital resources. No production is possible without all three, although the proportions in which they are mixed can, of course, vary greatly. In the simplest case, a subsistence farmer tilling the soil is using mainly labour and natural resources, but he still requires some fixed capital (in the form of simple farm buildings and implements) and some working capital (in the form of seeds and the food he saves to feed his family between harvests). At the opposite extreme, an automatic telephone exchange is nearly all capital, but nevertheless human hands built it, human hands keep it in repair and it is made of materials which, originally, were supplied by nature. In the case of service workers and administrators the relationship with capital and raw materials may not always be self-evident, but it is there if one sees them as part of the national labour force, depending for their employment on the continued production of economic goods. In the same way, the people we think of as "decision makers" are taking decisions, ultimately if not directly, about the use of capital, natural resources and labour. They are themselves a specialised type of worker, whose function is the organisation of economic resources.

Sound economic management consists of making the best use of the available resources. If one of these resources is in much more abundant supply than the other two, the decision makers will—or should—economise to the utmost their use of the two that are scarce. Unemployment occurs when one, or possibly two, of the resources is not available in sufficient quantities to support the third. A machine may stand idle because there are no skilled workers to operate it or because there is a shortage of raw materials to feed it; land may be unused because there is not enough labour to cultivate it or not enough capital to pay the workers' wages and furnish the required equipment. Men are unemployed when there is not enough land or capital, or both, with which to work.

Unemployment also occurs when there is no demand for the product of the enterprise, or for only a small part of it: and economic demand, one need hardly add, implies something more than human need. It calls for purchasing power—in the hands of the individual for personal or family expenditure, and in the coffers of the community for the provision of social services. In a country where the people and the government are very poor, demand obviously will not be strong. It is strengthened mainly by rising incomes, which are themselves the result of steady employment and improved productivity, both of which normally require both capital investment and increased supplies of raw materials. Thus the different factors react upon each other. If the economy is on the move, they stimulate each other; but if it is slowing down or barely in motion, they drag upon each other. In countries at a low level of development the process is often barely under way. Earnings generally are too low to stimulate demand or provide for investment; because of lack of demand and lack of investment, production is not high enough to raise incomes or generate new capital. So once again the problem in the poorer parts of the world is to break a vicious circle.

Who owns the land and the capital and how the market is governed are elements that differ from State to State, but social institutions cannot alter the basic forces. They may of course alter the availability of the needed resources, but it remains true that economic activity results from mixing the *available* resources in an effective manner. Today the governments of countries with mixed economies try to control the rate of economic activity, which is to a large degree reflected in the level of employment, by regulating consumer demand and investment. The position in the developing countries, however, is quite different. In principle, no doubt, it remains a matter of bringing together an effective combination of labour, land and capital and providing the desired degree of stimulation from the market; but in practice everything is out of phase from the beginning. There is an enormous supply of labour and a feeble flow of capital; in many cases there is also a chronic shortage of land, and practically everywhere there is a market that is nearly moribund—or rather, that has never come to life. How to bring the economy to life is exactly the problem facing the developing countries.

The problem is not the result of an economic recession (recession from what?), for whereas rich countries with rising unemployment rates may well worry about the need to revive the economy, in most parts of the Third World it is not so much a matter of economic revival as of economic birth. When there is a recession in an industrialised country, workers are unemployed, capital is unemployed and raw materials which could be obtained are un-employed. For some reason, the locomotive has run out of steam or jumped the tracks. Mass unemployment of workers in the Third World, on the other hand, may well be accompanied by full employment of available capital and, very often, full employment of the available land. The unemployed masses are men and women whom the locomotive has passed by. Evidently there were just too many of them to make the journey.

The late George Bernard Shaw, in his early days in the Fabian Society, never tired of pointing out that one of the peculiarities of labour is that it multiplies of its own accord, while capital has to be saved up (usually slowly) and the supply of land is limited by nature. He attributed much of the misery of industrial Britain in the nineteenth century to this idiosyncrasy. That was in a country whose labour force was growing by about 1 per cent per annum, with a capital/labour ratio higher than that of any other country in the world at the time, and able to draw on an Empire full of cheap raw materials. What would Shaw have thought of a modern so-called "devel-oping" country, with a labour force growing at 3 per cent per annum, a derisory capital/labour ratio and quite possibly a shortage of land? No doubt he would have given the advice that is now commonplace: such a country must make the fullest possible use of its human material, while building up its capital equipment and developing its natural resources.

The injunction to make the fullest use of human resources seems to beg the question. "We *are* your human resources", an unemployed crowd might well retort, when informed that the cure for their country's economic ailments is to make full use of its human potential. The new emphasis on human resources, however, as exemplified in the ILO World Employment Programme, does call for a different approach to economic planning in many countries, in which the search for ways and means of employing more labour more productively, on the land available and with the minimum capital investment, is given first priority. One way of doing this, as already indicated, is by raising the skills and technical knowledge of workers by training and guidance. This is itself a form of investment, the cost of which, as we have also seen, can be high enough to worry a government with meagre capital resources. The test is whether a given amount of capital invested in this way creates more employment—useful and lasting employment—than the same amount of capital invested in some other way.

There is no evading this question. Whatever methods are adopted for creating employment, some capital is always required. Opening up new lands to employ more people in the countryside (even if the land itself could be acquired and given away free of charge), starting rural industries, building access roads, cutting irrigation canals, however modest the outlay, however

Figure 10.   Projected growth of the labour force in Colombia and growth of employment
at recent rates

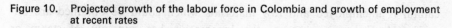

Millions

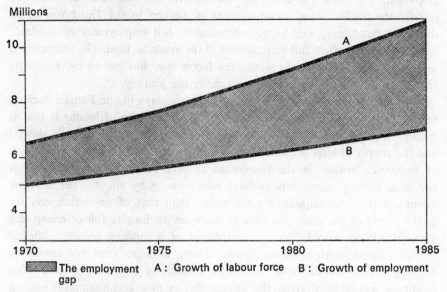

The employment   A : Growth of labour force   B : Growth of employment
gap

Source: based on ILO: *Towards full employment: a programme for Colombia* (Geneva, 1970).

labour-intensive the techniques employed ... none of this is possible without
drawing on the nation's capital resources.

A perfect example is provided by the Colombia employment mission's
proposal to expand the construction industry, a move which would involve
a very heavy investment of capital. The Colombia mission's case was simply
that investment in that industry would create more employment than a
comparable sum poured into certain other industries. Confronted with an
estimate that the Colombian labour force would probably grow from 6.5 million to 11 million in the following 15 years, with more than a million of them
unemployed at the start (see figure 10), the mission asked itself: where might
all these added millions of people be employed, with the lowest capital outlay,
on reasonable assumptions of what the market will accept? One of the
answers was a greatly expanded construction industry.

This approach, in fact, reverses the conventional planning priorities.
Instead of setting up output targets and then calculating what these would
require in capital investment and in skilled and unskilled manpower, the
mission put employment creation first and then indicated the investment
needed and the expected production growth that would follow. This it did
by scrutinising each sector of the economy in turn with a view to estimating
its employment potential relative to the market and to capital inputs. The

result was a tentative 15-year plan for full employment which, however, will still call for an enormous investment of capital.

CAPITAL FORMATION

It can be argued that a bigger labour force will generate more capital than a smaller one. Since capital is simply the part of the national output that is not consumed but is saved for purposes of expansion, this would be true if output per worker remained constant and if the national product consumed and saved remained the same. Under certain conditions there might possibly be a bigger amount left over for investment. What matters in practice is how much bigger and whether, in any case, it will be bigger relative to the size of the labour force. It would need to be very much bigger just to keep pace with current rates of population growth. How many extra goods are produced, how much extra capital?

Capital is, as we have seen, only one of the elements required for economic development, but it is a most important one. Out of its small fund of capital, the developing nation has to finance the new schools, new hospitals, new houses, new farms, extra workshops and other properties demanded by a rapidly increasing population, before it can devote anything to net economic development. It has been calculated that a developing country with a typical capital/output ratio will have to spend approximately 4 per cent of its national income on "demographic investment" for every 1 per cent of population growth. Demographic investment is defined for the purpose of this calculation as the sum of all the commitments necessitated by the increased population, including the appropriate proportion of the cost of land reclamation and industrial equipment needed to employ them. So a country with 2 per cent annual growth of population will have to divert 8 per cent of its total production to demographic investment, and a country with a 3 per cent growth (which is not uncommon) will have to allot 12 per cent. If capital formation in such a country represents 20 per cent of the national product, it will thus be compelled to devote three parts of its new capital resources to maintaining the existing standards of its rapidly expanding population, for every two parts it can spare for development. On this assumption, a high fertility country accumulating considerably less than 20 per cent would scarcely be developing at all, the whole of its additional capital resources being absorbed by demographic investment. A visitor might be impressed by what looked like a surge of development. Schools, hospitals, houses, factories, farm buildings could be going up everywhere: yet the country would be standing still. All these new installations would be counterbalanced by population growth. Only a strong injection of outside aid could possibly remedy the situation, and that obviously is no answer in the long run.

Under the same assumptions a fall in fertility would have the reverse effect. A reduction of 1 per cent in the population growth rate would release 4 per cent of the country's total production for genuine development. A simple calculation thus shows that if the figures were the not unusual ones of 3 per cent population growth and 20 per cent capital formation, of which 12 per cent went to demographic investment and 8 per cent to all other investment, a reduction of 1 per cent in fertility would raise the capital resources available for net development by 50 per cent. Greatly increased resources could be released for employment creation—and, moreover, fewer jobs would eventually be required.

These figures are admittedly hypothetical, though based on fairly typical conditions and realistic assumptions. They are also borne out by specific studies. Mahmoud Seklani, for example, in a detailed paper contributed to the 1965 World Population Conference, calculated the demographic investment required by the Tunisian Development Plan (1962-71) as 42 per cent of all investment or 10 to 11 per cent of the national production. His calculations were based on an annual population growth rate of 2.6 per cent. Thus, in this case, each percentage point of population growth would in fact absorb the 4 per cent of the national product suggested by the hypothesis. Tunisia aimed at a high capital formation rate of 26 per cent at the end of the period. At that rate demographic investment would absorb 40 per cent of all investment on the basis of the hypothetical equation, a figure very close to the 42 per cent of Seklani's calculations.

SOME CALCULATIONS

Felix Paukert, in an article published in the *International Labour Review* in May 1965, examined among other things the effect of population growth on investment in 12 industrialised countries and 21 developing countries, on the basis of their actual record over a period of time averaging about seven years (see figure 11). His purpose was to show the manner in which the increase in the national income was spent. For this purpose, the total increase was divided into the share required to offset population growth, the share absorbed by government services, the share that went in consumption—indicating the rise in living standards—and the balance devoted to investment. At one extreme were countries like Austria, with a practically stable population growing by less than 0.25 per cent per annum, which devoted 32 per cent of its increased income to investment and where only 2.6 per cent was needed to provide for its slowly increasing population; and at the other extreme were three developing countries where the share taken by population growth greatly exceeded 100 per cent. In other words,

Figure 11. Gains from economic development

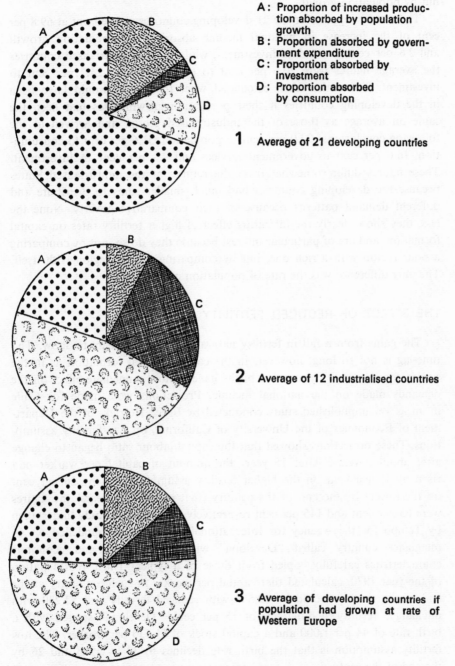

A : Proportion of increased produc-
    tion absorbed by population
    growth
B : Proportion absorbed by govern-
    ment expenditure
C : Proportion absorbed by
    investment
D : Proportion absorbed
    by consumption

1 Average of 21 developing countries

2 Average of 12 industrialised countries

3 Average of developing countries if
population had grown at rate of
Western Europe

Source: based on Felix Paukert: "The distribution of gains from economic development", in *International Labour Review* (Geneva, ILO), Vol. 91, No. 5, May 1965.

the whole of their increased output, and more besides, had been cancelled out by population growth.

The average figures for the 21 developing countries worked out at 69.8 per cent of the increase in national income absorbed by population growth and 2.6 per cent devoted to investment, while in the industrialised countries the average figures were 20.6 per cent to population and 24.7 per cent to investment. The author then calculated what the results would have been in the developing countries if their population growth rates had been the same on average as those of the industrialised group, and arrived at the following conclusions: 22.0 per cent to population, 51.6 per cent to consumption, 16.6 per cent to government services and 9.8 per cent to investment. These figures differ somewhat from the returns of the industrialised States because the developing countries had much smaller sums to distribute and different demand patterns because of their comparative poverty. None the less, they show clearly the inhibiting effect of higher fertility rates on capital formation, and are of particular interest because they do so, not by comparing a poor region with a rich one, but by comparing a poor region with itself. The only difference was the rate of population growth.

THE EFFECT OF REDUCED FERTILITY

The gains from a fall in fertility naturally take some years to show. The time-lag is not so long, however, in the case of capital formation as in the size of the labour force, because births have a more immediate effect on the demands made on the national income. Projections were made for Chile in an as yet unpublished study conducted by Bruce Herrick, of the Department of Economics of the University of California, on two fertility assumptions. These projections showed that the capital/labour ratio began to change after about 5 years. After 15 years the amount of capital per worker had risen by 15 per cent on the higher fertility assumption and by 26 per cent on the lower; by the end of the century (that is, after 35 years) the figures were 65 per cent and 145 per cent respectively. The massive study undertaken by Tempo for the Agency for International Development, modelled on an imaginary country called "Developa" with demographic and economic characteristics carefully copied from those of a typical Third World nation of the year 1970, calculated that capital per worker in such a country at the end of the century would be $2,580 with reduced fertility and $2,230 with unchanged fertility, a difference of 15 per cent. "Developa" started with a birth rate of 44 per 1,000 and a capital stock of $1,630 per worker. The low fertility assumption is that the birth rate declines to 30 by 1985 and 26 by the end of the century.

Professor B. Thomas Walsh, of the University of Pittsburgh, has calculated the effect of four different fertility rates on economic development in Jamaica, starting from the year 1970. His highest assumption is the usual no-change formula; his lowest is that fertility declines steadily to a point, about the year 2000, when the population is just replacing itself. The other two assumptions are spaced in between. Among other things, Walsh worked out the percentage of the national product that would have to be invested over a series of five-year periods to maintain the average level of output per person. Inasmuch as merely to maintain that level spells economic stagnation, his figures are obviously an underestimate of the investment needed for progress. At the highest fertility rate the investment required simply to maintain standards is 14.76 per cent of the national product for 1975-80, and at the lowest rate it is 11.44 per cent. Twenty years later, when the fertility drop has begun to tell, the percentages are 15.44 per cent and 2.24 per cent respectively, and after another 20 years the figure is still much the same on the high fertility assumption but has fallen nearly to zero on the lowest assumption.

Some of these figures are obviously over-precise—the result, no doubt, of computerising the basic data—but they all point in the same direction. In countries that are poor to begin with, rapid population growth is a heavy drag on capital formation, and therefore on employment promotion. This is not surprising when one considers that capital has to be saved out of current production, whether expressed in personal incomes, government revenues or company profits. Most developing countries have relatively few business corporations, so that aggregate savings from this source are bound to be low, no matter how conscientious individual firms may be in ploughing earnings back into the enterprise, or the government in taxing profits. Often, indeed, a part of a company's earnings may have to be sent out of the country to recompense foreign investors. At the same time most families are too large and too poor to save, and for the same reason the government's taxation opportunities are limited at this level. There must be many families, in fact, which financially represent a net loss to the State, since they are receiving more in public services than they contribute in taxation. On the other hand, at the upper end of the social scale the public revenues are often minimised by unprogressive taxation systems and widespread tax evasion. And when the government has finally acquired a little capital, much of it is already earmarked for the new schools, new hospitals and expanded services of many kinds required by the swelling multitude.

THE SWELLING ARMY OF WORKERS

Meanwhile, nothing can stop the working population of the Third World from expanding rapidly for many years to come. Even an unexpectedly swift decline in fertility could have only a long-term effect. On the United Nations medium fertility assumption, the population of the world's less developed regions aged 15 to 64 will grow from 1,400 million to 2,100 million between 1970 and 1985, an increase of 50 per cent. During the same period the population of working age in the more developed regions will grow from approximately 700 million to 800 million, an increase of only 15 per cent. Beyond 1985 any change in fertility which may have begun in 1970 will begin to show, albeit gradually. Even at the end of the century, the whole of the population over 30 years of age will, after all, consist of persons born before 1970. This delayed effect makes it more imperative, if anything, to take early action.

Estimates of the numbers who will be in need of employment are more complicated than those of the working-age population, because they must take into account the extent to which different sections of the community actually want to work, and this changes with circumstances. Housewives, full-time students and the disabled are normally excluded from the economically active population. The unemployed are counted, on the assumption that they are part of the labour supply; but as more jobs become available the labour force still tends to grow because many persons who otherwise would not try to obtain work begin to apply for employment. The growth in the numbers of married women in the labour force in many countries since the Second World War is a striking example of this tendency.

The labour force projections prepared by the International Labour Office as part of the integrated demographic researches of the United Nations indicate a net increase in the world labour force of over 450 million workers, or approximately one-third, between 1970 and 1985 (see table 5). Of this total, 290 million will be in Asia, 55 million in Africa, 42 million in Latin America and the remaining 70 million in Europe, North America, the USSR, Australia and New Zealand combined. For every 100 workers in need of employment in Africa in 1970 there will be 142 only 15 years later; for every 100 in Asia there will be 134 in 1985; and for every 100 in Latin America there will be 148. As for the rest of the world, containing the great bulk of the more developed areas, the estimated labour force in 1985 is put at 116 per cent of the 1970 figure. In Western Europe the estimate is 109 per cent.

As we saw in Chapter 6, the Ministry of Planning and Employment in Sri Lanka made labour force projections on three different fertility assumptions. Starting with an actual labour force of 4.10 million in 1968, the three projections for 1983 ranged only between 6.32 million and 6.33 million, which is what one would expect after 15 years; but by 1998 the spread was from 8.31 million to 9.34 million. Thus, for every 100 workers in Ceylon

Table 5. Anticipated growth of the labour force in 15 years (millions)

Country	1970	1985	Percentage increase
Argentina	8.87	10.49	18
Burma	12.16	15.97	32
France	21.94	24.55	12
India	222.69	305.65	37
Ivory Coast	2.30	3.16	37
Jamaica	0.65	0.93	43
Japan	52.22	59.52	14
Kenya	4.35	6.72	54
Mexico	14.31	22.99	61
Morocco	4.16	6.52	57
USSR	123.30	147.40	19
United States	81.58	101.84	25
Africa	*132*	*187*	*42*
Asia	*857*	*1 146*	*34*
Latin America	*88*	*130*	*48*
Rest of world	*435*	*502*	*16*

Source: ILO: *Labour force projections 1965-1985* (Geneva, 1971).

requiring employment in 1968 there would, 30 years later, be 223 at the higher rate of population growth and 202 at the lower.

Professor Walsh, in his Jamaican study, projected the size of the labour force on four different fertility assumptions, starting in 1965 (see figure 12). At the highest fertility rate—which, in effect, assumed no fall from the existing level—he estimated that there would be an increase of 240 per cent in the number of workers by the end of the century, compared with 196 per cent at the lowest rate. At a date 20 years later, when practically the whole of the 1965 labour force would have been replaced, he estimated an increase of 637 per cent at the highest rate and 237 at the lowest. Thus, for every 100 workers requiring employment in 1967 there would be 737 on the unchanged fertility assumption 53 years later and 337 if fertility declined in the manner described earlier. The Tempo study found that the labour force of the imaginary country "Developa", set at 3.62 million in 1970 (out of a total population of 10 million), would grow in 30 years to 9.11 million with unchanged fertility and to 8.32 million if fertility declined steadily from 44 per 1,000 to 26 per 1,000 through the three decades. Thus such a country would have to find employment for 800,000 more workers on the one fertility assumption than it would on the other. In either case, the employment load is formidable.

Figure 12.   Projected growth of Jamaica's labour force on different assumptions (1967 = 100)

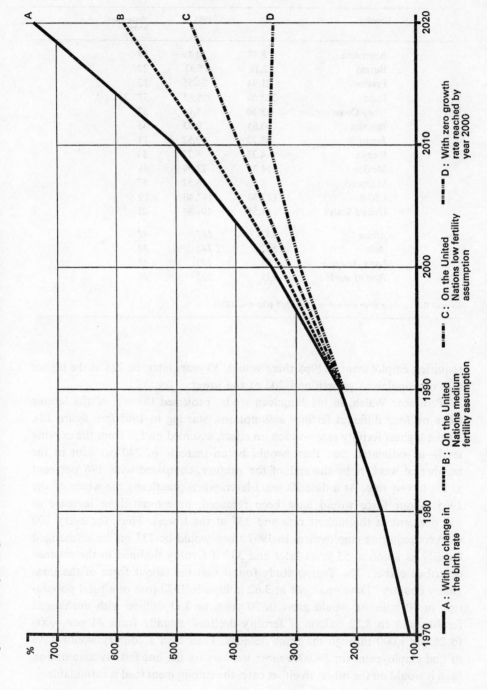

Source: based on R. Thomas Walsh: *Economic development and population control: a 50-year projection for Jamaica* (New York, Praeger, 1971).

All these labour force projections suffer inevitably from the complexities of estimating in advance how many persons of the two sexes and in the different age-groups will actually seek employment. Professor Walsh assumes for the purpose of his demonstration that participation rates will remain the same, age for age and by sex, throughout the period of his projections. Experience suggests that this assumption builds into the equation an upward bias, but for the purpose of Walsh's calculations—which was to show the effect of different fertility rates on the future size of the labour force—this is a secondary consideration; his aim was to discover what that effect would be over a given period of time if all other factors remained constant. The purpose of the International Labour Office projections is somewhat different: they are an attempt to forecast what the size of the labour force will actually be in the different countries of the world, at a date in the future. The current series therefore stop at 1985, and they allow for the increasing numbers of young people who may be expected to stay on at schools and colleges, for the emancipation of women, and for various other factors which also have to be projected into the future on the basis of past and present experience. If anybody should come across these various estimates 30 years from now, therefore, he may find that they have not been precisely confirmed by history. None the less, however wide the margin of error may eventually prove to be, four conclusions may be stated as being almost self-evident. Firstly, a country with a very high birth rate will normally have a rapidly growing labour force, though the population and the labour force may not be growing at the same speed (only disaster or an abnormal migration rate can upset this relationship). Secondly, a decline in fertility will have no immediate effect on the size of the labour force, but—thirdly—after about 20 years the effect will be increasingly marked. Fourthly, the amount of capital available per worker will tend to grow more slowly with rapid population growth. This, in itself, will hamper employment, and it will do so without delay.

THE PROSPECT FOR YOUTH

It is the young people who are the first to be left out in the cold. In a high fertility situation, the labour force naturally grows fastest in the lower age-groups. Out of an estimated 180 million additional jobs to be found in Asia during the Second Development Decade, 34 million will be required by workers aged 15 to 24, notwithstanding a considerable increase in the proportion of young people staying on at school or college. In Africa 9 million out of 33 million will be of that age, and in Latin America 7 million out of 25 million. These, it should be remembered, are the fertility increment, the surplus over the number of workers of that age at the beginning of the decade. The actual number of young workers expected to join the labour force at the age of 15 during the ten years is about 270 million in Asia, approaching 50 million in Africa and more than 30 million in Latin America.

Not surprisingly, unemployment is already heaviest among the young. The ILO mission to Colombia found that young people under 25 accounted for more than 60 per cent of total urban unemployment and workers under 35 for nearly 82 per cent. More than a quarter of all workers under 25 were out of work. The mission to Sri Lanka, in turn, found that at the beginning of 1970 young people aged 15 to 24 comprised 82 per cent of all openly unemployed persons in that country. Moreover, in a country with a labour force at that time of almost 4 million, 250,000 young people were leaving school every year. Open unemployment in Sri Lanka among persons aged 15 to 24 who had successfully completed secondary school was 70 per cent in the towns and "higher still in rural areas and among women".

In Kenya it has been estimated that in 1965 more than 60,000 out of a total of 160,000 school leavers were unable to obtain employment. The Kenya Development Plan for 1970-74 anticipates a growth in the labour force of 830,000 during the five-year period, of whom about 650,000 will be school leavers. Wage earners and the self-employed are expected to increase in numbers by 405,000 in the five years: the rest will have to work on the family farm, if they can get work at all. In Tanzania it was anticipated that 250,000 young people aged 15 would join the labour force in 1970, of whom 60,000 would be primary school leavers; at the same time it was expected that only 11,000 new non-agricultural jobs would be created. A survey conducted in Nigeria in the years following independence (i.e. the early 1960s) among youths who had been to school revealed that only 29 per cent of the primary school leavers were in full-time employment, 6 per cent had odd jobs and 65 per cent were wholly unemployed. Of the unemployed, 54 per cent had been out of work for more than a year and 15 per cent for more than three years. The returns for youths with secondary education were somewhat better, but only 47 per cent of them were in full-time employment.

A report on unemployment in metropolitan towns in Malaysia revealed that in 1965 something like 90 per cent of the unemployed aged 15 to 19 had never had a job and more than 60 per cent of those aged 20 to 25 were still looking for their first opening. These two groups together constituted 75 per cent of all the unemployed in the major towns. Later figures given in the Second Malaysia Plan (1971-75) indicated that this situation had, if anything, deteriorated. A full 65 per cent of all unemployed—rural and urban—in West Malaysia in 1967 were new jobseekers, compared with 47 per cent only five years previously. As the authors of the Plan pointed out, unemployment in West Malaysia is largely a youth phenomenon.

The national youth services to be found in most developing countries help to keep a number of young people out of the labour market for a certain period, although this is not generally their main purpose. The direct benefit derived by the member is often psychological. In most organisations of this kind the young men and women concerned have the satisfaction of carrying out some pioneer tasks of benefit to the nation, such as road building, land clearance, swamp reclamation and the construction of airstrips. They also improve their education and receive a certain amount of basic training for the future, particularly in agriculture and animal husbandry. They see something of their country and develop a sense of nationhood and community service. In a few cases, they learn arms drill to become the nucleus of a national militia. Whatever the form of service, they are spared for a time the chagrin of searching for a job that does not exist.

The value of this relief should not be underestimated. It takes the pressure off these young people and off society at a critical time for both. When they have completed their period in the national youth service, perhaps more of them will return to their villages and fewer will sink into the city slums than might otherwise have been the case. The search for work has to begin sooner or later, but it is better a little later. Apart from the services rendered by the youth corps, a part of the employment load is taken off the economy.

In countries with low fertility rates, most of the young people entering the labour market step into vacancies created by the retirement of older workers; not, of course, into exactly the same positions, but into places that have become available at the beginning of the column as the workforce steadily moves on. Even allowing for technological changes in the nature of employment, this is broadly true. In higher fertility countries, on the other hand, the employment phalanx is very narrow at one end and very wide at the other; there are comparatively few older workers retiring, while increasing numbers of young people join the end of the line. As a consequence, it can be estimated that between 50 and 70 per cent of all new entrants to the labour force in the Third World require newly created openings.

THE WIDENING GAP

Because the capital-starved economy has failed to expand rapidly enough and in the right direction to create new openings at this back-breaking pace, mass unemployment is spreading. The Colombia mission found that the labour force was growing by at least 3.5 per cent per year and employment by 2.3 per cent. Result: unemployment mounting by 100,000 a year. The mission to Sri Lanka looked wistfully backwards and said: "Suppose that a family planning campaign policy had been implemented at the same time as the malaria eradication campaign in the 1940s and had reached the present target birth rate of 25 per 1,000 in 1955.[1] The result today of such a programme would have been to lighten the task of creating employment very considerably; in fact, past trends in employment would be about sufficient, if continued, to reach full employment in the 1980s. In a sense, therefore, the magnitude of the task now facing [Sri Lanka] is due to the failure to limit births in the first post-war decades."

As it is, the labour force in Sri Lanka is now growing by about 3 per cent per year. Employment in the 1960s grew by less than 2 per cent a year, and had almost certainly slowed down to a much slower rate in the last years of the decade, though the figure was not accurately known. Result: more than a quarter of the entire labour force is expected to be out of work "well before 1980" if the process is not arrested. Bearing in mind the need to find work for the existing unemployed, the mission in fact estimated that jobs would have to be created at a rate close to 4 per cent a year to attain full employment (that is, employment for 95 per cent of the labour force) by 1983. That is double the present rate.

The Second Malaysia Plan (1971-75) stated: "The pace of new job creation could not keep up with the strong spurt in labour supply during the First Malaysia Plan period. As a result, unemployment [in West Malaysia] rose from about 180,000 or 6.5 per cent of the labour force at the start of the period, to about 250,000 or about 8 per cent at its close in 1970." Observe that this is an increase in the actual numbers of unemployed of some 40 per cent. In fact the labour force in West Malaysia grew at an annual rate of 2.9 per cent during the period, while employment grew at a rate of 2.6 per cent, by no means a discreditable performance. Assuming that this rate of job creation could be maintained and that the labour force would grow approximately at the same rate as the population as a whole, these figures suggest that a fall of 0.3 per cent in the rate of natural increase of the population would be sufficient to bring the two into line. If there was a steeper decline, the employment gap would begin to close.

FERTILITY AND WORKING WOMEN

A question that has been much discussed in recent years is the effect of fertility on the employment of women and vice versa. A paper presented by B. T. Urlanis to the 1965 World Population Conference argued strongly that women's participation in employment on the same terms as men led to

---

[1] The aim is to reduce the rate from the 1965 level of 35 per 1,000 to 25 per 1,000 in 1975.

a lowering of the birth rate, saying that among the social factors influencing the birth rate the first which deserved note was the social position of women. Urlanis gave figures showing that the birth rate in the USSR was approximately 50 per cent higher among dependent women than among working women, except among teenagers. In the most prolific 20-29 age-group, the birth rate was 138 per 1,000 working women and 199 per 1,000 dependent women. From these facts Urlanis concluded that the influx of women into social labour was a material factor in the decline of the birth rate. An alternative explanation is that women with fewer children find it easier to go out to work, or simply that a society in which women have more opportunities for employment is in any case likely to be a relatively emancipated one, in which birth control is more likely to be practised; but the view that employment curtails fertility now seems to be widely accepted. Thus a seminar on population and manpower problems held in Bangkok in January 1971, under the joint auspices of the ILO and the United Nations Economic Commission for Asia and the Far East, passed a resolution calling on the organisers to examine the inter-relationship between fertility and the employment of women, in order to assess the efficacy of encouraging increased participation of women in the labour force as a means of reducing fertility. It should be noted that most women in the region work, but they work on the land or in the home. The allusion is evidently to wage employment.

A survey entitled "Some demographic aspects of female employment in Eastern Europe and the USSR" by Jerzy Berent of the United Nations Economic Commission for Europe, which appeared in the *International Labour Review* in February 1970, contained several pages of informative tables which demonstrated that in the seven countries covered, whatever the age of the worker or the field of employment, the fewer children a woman had the more likely she was to be in paid employment. This is what one would expect, but it does not by itself resolve the condundrum of cause and effect. A more recent study, submitted by Léon Tabah to the Council of Europe's Second European Population Conference at Strasbourg in September 1971, states: "Fertility in working women is considerably lower than that in women not at work [. . .] although it is not really known which is cause and which effect. The indications are in fact that both factors are at work: women so far not particularly fertile find it easier to take a job, and this same low fertility rate is then very likely to continue, in order for them to keep their job and thus their independence, or to take it up again without too many family difficulties. It may be argued that this process is largely responsible for the drop in fertility in Europe."

In a paper entitled "Fertility trends in Europe since the Second World War", Professor David Glass calls for more research into this question.

"The statistics for Norway, Switzerland and England and Wales", he points out, "show that the economically active women constitute a very important element in differential fertility. Indeed, in England and Wales such women exhibit a lower fertility as a group than any of the 17 socio-economic categories into which the husband's employment is classified. This kind of situation suggests that much more attention should be—and should have been— given to the analysis of married women's employment in fertility censuses, and also that it would be eminently worth while undertaking a study of the impact of such employment on over-all trends in fertility since the 1930s." Thus Professor Glass is not willing to commit himself as to the nature of the interaction, in the absence of fuller information. The facts, however, are not in dispute.

HOW MANY UNEMPLOYED ?

How many unemployed are there in the world today? The total cannot be computed, but on any showing it must be a staggering sum. In 1969 the President of the World Bank, Robert S. McNamara, gave a figure of one in five of the entire male labour force of the developing world. That would be 120 million, not counting the women. Most official unemployment returns refer only to wage earners, who constitute a small minority of the workers in most parts of the Third World. In Botswana they comprise 8 per cent of the labour force, in Ghana 20, in Morocco 35; in Bolivia 30, in Brazil 48; in India 13. Labour ministry returns frequently show only the numbers reporting at an employment exchange, a formality many of the chronically unemployed consider time-wasting, and they often exclude anybody who works even for a few hours a week. In India, for example, a worker gainfully occupied for one hour a day is officially listed as employed.

Attempts can be made to count these underemployed workers as an appropriate fraction of the wholly unemployed; two men working half time, for example, can be regarded as one employed and one unemployed. The Colombia mission, taking urban underemployment into account in this way, put the effective number of unemployed in that country in 1970 as the equivalent of 1.5 million workers, against 5 million in employment in town and field. That was more than 20 per cent of the labour force; yet the official figures were 4.9 per cent for the country as a whole at the 1964 census and 9.6 per cent for Bogotá in 1969. The mission did not attempt to estimate underemployment on the land.

Governments of developing countries that have made a frank attempt to assess their unemployment burden have usually uncovered a grim situation. The Pakistan National Manpower Council put the open unemployed at 20 per cent of the labour force in 1965, or about 7.5 million workers out of 37 million. It was hoped to create some 5.5 million additional jobs in the following Five-Year Plan period (1966-70), yet such was the effect of high fertility that more than 4 million of the hoped-for new openings would be swamped by the growth in the labour force. During India's Third Five-Year Plan (1961-66) no fewer than 14.5 million new jobs were created, but the labour force grew by 17 million. Unemployment at the beginning of the period was already assessed at about 10 million, so over the five years the economy would in fact have had to create 27 million extra jobs to close the gap, at a rate of 100,000 a week. No estimates of unemployment are given in the current Fourth Five-Year Plan (1969-74), since a committee was formed in 1968 to examine the bases on which the figures should be computed; but there can be no doubt that population pressure has continued to frustrate the Indian Government's efforts to reduce the number of the unemployed. The original draft of the Fourth Five-Year Plan (1966-71) put the expected growth of the labour force during that period at 23 million and the likely increase in employment at 19.5 million: another 3.5 million added to the queue. Not surprisingly, the ILO's Asian Regional Conference in 1968 adopted a resolution which stated that there could be no lasting solution of employment problems in most Asian countries unless the current high rate of population growth was reduced. And growth rates are even higher in most parts of Africa and Latin America. . . .

At the beginning of the First United Nations Development Decade in 1960 it was widely assumed that if the countries of the Third World achieved high rates of economic growth the employment problem would take care of itself. This was found to be an illusion as country after country passed the target of 5 per cent annual economic growth and reported rapidly increasing numbers of unemployed. On the basis of the results in a representative number of countries, the United Nations Expert Committee on Development Planning calculated that the higher the rate of economic growth, the more rapidly the employment gap had actually widened—a paradoxical conclusion which is the exact opposite of the one predicted at the beginning of the Decade. The explanation of this apparent contradiction is that much of the rapid growth had been achieved by the installation of sophisticated capital equipment which boosted production in sectors of the economy employing few workers while the national labour force was advancing remorselessly along the line. A new approach to development planning, which takes into account the high labour/capital ratio typical of an economy with a rapidly expanding workforce and limited investment resources, is therefore necessary if the trend is to be reversed. At the same time, a reduction in fertility would in due course reduce the pressure from below.

The Colombia mission observed: "The double task of reducing unemployment and catching up with a labour force growth of some 3.5 per cent a year is so formidable that it will—if it can be managed at all—strain the country's economic and political capacity to the limit. This problem will start to seem less tremendous only about 15 years after a really sharp decline in fertility commences, which would require an official birth control policy with the full resources of the official medical services behind it. If no such decline occurs in the 1970s, the problem of unemployment will indeed look daunting in the mid-1980s." And the mission to Sri Lanka, after the passage quoted above, went on to say: "Well into the 1980s the growth of the labour force will be determined by the high birth rate and low infant mortality rates of the 1950s and 1960s. Its inexorable increase sets a pace that makes full employment very hard to achieve. [. . .] Will another employment mission in 1985 be saying: 'If only there had been a vigorous official policy in the 1970s, using the full resources of health services to achieve a birth rate of 25 per 1,000 by 1975, the prospects for reducing unemployment in the year 2000 would not look so bleak'?"

RURAL EMPLOYMENT

10

Between 1970 and the end of the century the rural population of the less developed regions of the world is expected to grow by some 1,000 million persons, after allowing for migration to the towns of approximately half the natural increase. That is to say, without the anticipated migration the growth would be nearer 2,000 million. Of the expected net increase, 230 million are forecast for Africa and nearly 700 million for southern Asia, principally in Bangladesh, India, Indonesia and Pakistan. If these estimates are proved correct, the rural economies of Africa and southern Asia, which already in many areas are yielding the barest subsistence to the population, will have to support nearly twice as many people only 30 years from now as they do today. In Latin America, where urbanisation is already well advanced, the rural areas will still have to support 32 million more people at the end of the century, or four for every three they support today.

While it is true that the labour force does not increase as an exact ratio of the total population, the labour participation rates are not likely to change very much over two or three decades. These figures, therefore, indicate the need for an enormous expansion of rural employment.

This would be a sufficiently sobering prospect if the rural areas of the Third World were bathed in prosperity, with the labour force busily engaged in a thriving economy. As things are, the effort of developing the country-side so as to provide the needed employment is handicapped from the start by the heavy arrears to be made up before any real advance can be made. Apart from the low earnings of the workers who are in employment, millions are already unemployed and millions more are underemployed. Estimates based on the 1961 census and the National Sample Survey in India put the number of open rural unemployed at 8 million at that time, nearly half of them under the age of 27. During the following five years approximately 4 million additional jobs were created in the rural areas of India but the rural labour force grew by more than 12 million (many of these, however, would be occupied after a fashion on the family farm). No official estimate was made of underemployment, except for those who actually sought part-time jobs.

In countries with a sizeable plantation economy the prospects of the wage earners on the big estates are equally depressed by population growth. Outside the plantations, open unemployment on the land in Sri Lanka averaged 10 to 12 per cent between 1963 and 1968. Although the plantation labour force was made up of some 675,000 workers in 1970, roughly four rural workers out of five (2.5 million in all) still work on small farms, either as owners or tenants, with a few self-employed craftsmen in the villages. This is the pattern of rural labour in most of the Third World. In Indonesia some 19.5 million workers out of approximately 25 million in the sector comprising agriculture, forestry, hunting and fishing were either working on their own or as family workers, at the last count. In Iran the figures were 2.4 million out of 3.2 million, in Ghana 1.4 million out of 1.6 million, in Brazil 8.7 million out of 11.7 million, and so on. Moreover, this sector is generally by far the biggest in the economy. In India, for example, it accounts for more than 70 per cent of all workers. In few developing countries does it comprise less than 50 per cent of the whole. The measurement of agricultural unemployment and underemployment in these circumstances is an almost impossible task. The figures given above for India are thus but the tip of an iceberg.

THE SCOURGE OF UNDEREMPLOYMENT

The effect of rapid population growth in the rural areas is more likely to take the form of underemployment than open unemployment, in the generally accepted sense of "persons known to be seeking work". The family grows, but the family plot remains the same. Unless the family obtains more land or learns radically improved techniques, the bigger workforce goes on working with the same supply of land and capital—a perfect illustration of how to create unemployment. If the plot is shared between the farmer's sons on his death, it is steadily divided into ever smaller fragments as the generations go by. If it is left intact to the eldest son, either he continues allowing the others to share such employment as it offers or they go away to swell the ranks of landless labourers, unless indeed they have long since quit the country to try their luck in the town.

Underemployment on the land is already widespread in most developing countries, though it is difficult to assess its extent. The fourteenth round of India's National Sample Survey (1958-59) put the numbers of known underemployed at 11 million for those of the rural workforce who reported available for additional work for up to 29 hours a week and 17 million for those available for additional work for 15 hours a week, but this was almost certainly an understatement of the real gravity of the problem. This estimate is in fact the lowest of four assessments of underemployment in India quoted by Sunil Guha in his book *Rural manpower and capital formation in India* (1969). The highest is a figure of 70 million given by V. L. Mehta for 1959, for "persons having work of less than half a day in a week on average in rural India". The total rural population of India at that time was about 350 million. Ten years later it was 430 million, notwithstanding migration to the towns. Most families would still be farming the same patch of ground.

According to Egypt's First Five-Year Plan a quarter of all male agricultural workers in that country in 1960, or more than a million men in all, were surplus to requirements. Reliable estimates indicate that rural workers in Morocco spend an average of 150 days a year in idleness. A survey in Madagascar found that the average number of days worked in a year varied from as little as 43 in some areas to 216 in others. The Inter-American Committee for Agricultural Development, after studying six Latin American countries, estimated that the 4.4 million agricultural workers employed on small farms in those countries would have to be cut to 700,000 if an economic labour/land ratio were to be reached. In other words, 37 workers out of 44 were really redundant.

The small amount of land per worker in densely populated countries with meagre capital resources is an obvious factor in the widespread unemployment and underemployment among farmworkers of the developing world. In very few Asian countries does the average area of arable land per worker exceed 1 hectare, and the ratio is falling all the time as the population rises. In India in 1961 it averaged 1.18 hectares, in Pakistan 1.15 hectares and in Indonesia 0.75 hectare. The mission to Sri Lanka observed that "the shortage of cultivable land in relation to population could be described as a major cause of unemployment".

Although smaller farms tend to be more intensively cultivated, population pressure can be so heavy that more than half the family labour is not really needed. A survey in Bombay state (now Maharashtra and Gujarat) showed that 68 per cent of workers on the smallest farms were superfluous, while even on the bigger farms the percentage was 16. This was some years ago, but the position today will, if anything, be worse, as a consequence of the high rate of natural increase. These figures were calculated by taking the total output of the farms and estimating how many hands would actually be needed to produce that amount, working normal hours on holdings of the same size without any improvement in technology. Unless they sought part-time employment elsewhere, these superfluous workers on the family farm would not be numbered in any official statistics.

In many parts of Latin America population growth puts a strain on the capacity of the small farm, while vast areas of uncultivated or slightly cultivated land remain thinly populated. Many studies have been published on this subject. The Colombian Land Reform Agency, for example, calculated that 940,000 out of 1.37 million families—seven out of every ten—depending on agriculture in Colombia in 1960 had either no land at all (175,000 families) or occupied a farm too small to provide adequate employment for two persons at the prevailing level of techniques. Another 361,000 families worked land capable of employing between two and four workers, and these were assumed to be effectively occupied. Meanwhile, the population went on expanding. Ten years later, notwithstanding migration to the towns, the Inter-American Committee for Agricultural Development estimated that the number of Colombian families with no land or not enough to employ the available family labour would have risen to 1.1 million—in other words, by about 160,000.

INEQUITABLE LAND DISTRIBUTION

At the same time, vast estates are owned by a tiny minority of big landowners, not only in Colombia but in other parts of the continent. The Inter-American Committee, after the study of six Latin American countries on which it based the estimate of underemployment already quoted, calculated that, if only half the land belonging to large estates in those countries were cultivated with the same labour intensity as the small farms, another 25 million workers could be absorbed, though presumably at a low level of activity. As already mentioned, the Committee estimated that only about one-sixth (700,000 out of 4.4 million) of the existing labour force was effectively employed. If a more economic size of farm were established, the extra land would therefore presumably provide a satisfactory livelihood for approximately 4 million (one-sixth of 25 million) workers, without any technological improvement. Since the present holdings are adequate for 700,000 workers, the total that could be effectively employed, if only half the land occupied by the big estates were distributed, approaches 5 million, or something like seven times the present number.

In such countries it can be argued that the problem is not population growth but land distribution. To the extent that this is so, the crucial question is whether new farms can be obtained and the necessary buildings and equipment provided fast enough to meet the needs of the rapidly expanding population—the race against time in another form. This is not the place to discuss the political difficulties involved in a radical policy of land reform, except to make the point, in passing, that they are exacerbated by population pressure. It has been repeatedly demonstrated that the land now locked up in big estates, even where it is under cultivation, could support a bigger population. The Inter-American Committee for Agricultural Development found that output per unit of land in Colombia, for example, was ten times as great on the smallest class of farms as on larger farms employing 12 or more workers—yet the smallest farms were still too tiny to support a family.

There have been cases where land reform has been followed, at least in the short run, by falling output, but they are the exceptions. In Bolivia, Chile, Japan, Mexico and Yugoslavia, average output per hectare increased substantially after land reform. In Kenya, where the famous "White Highlands" had been farmed on an impressive scale by European settlers using the most sophisticated modern equipment, the 1 million acres resettled after independence were producing approximately double the previous output within a few years, and were supporting about 250,000 persons, including some hired hands. The new farmers were using labour-intensive techniques to grow generally the same type of produce as the former owners. These results appear to dispose of the argument that land reform does not create productive employment but merely puts more hands to work producing the same or smaller harvests.

THE GREEN REVOLUTION

In some quarters the coming of the Green Revolution has been hailed as a providential answer to the rural employment problem, possibly rendering land reform unnecessary, at any rate on a radical scale. Others have argued that land reform is essential to the success of the Green Revolution, for both social and economic reasons.

The Green Revolution is the outcome of the Mexican researches of Norman E. Borlaug, the winner of the 1970 Nobel Peace Prize, who developed new varieties of high-yielding seed capable of producing 2,000 kilograms or more of wheat per hectare in place of the 800 or 900 kilograms customary in tropical countries. The introduction of this type of seed, both for wheat and rice, began on a large scale in south east Asia in 1966-67, and within three years it accounted for 40 per cent of the wheat acreage in India, 50 per cent in Nepal and 46 per cent in Pakistan. By the same time 40 per cent of the ricefields in the Philippines and 23 per cent in Malaysia had also been planted with high-yielding varieties. Apart from the respite the Green Revolution may bring to a world short of food, it has the great attraction that labour-intensive techniques can be employed to cultivate the new strains. Given the necessary training, a small farmer can increase his yields as readily as the biggest landowner.

This, however, hardly disposes of the need for land reform. In the first place, as we have seen, the majority of family holdings in many countries are so small that even with double the output and twice the amount of work they could still not adequately employ the adult members of the family. (Actually, it has been estimated that the increased labour requirements necessitated by the Green Revolution might be about 60 per cent.) In the second place, millions of landless peasants still look to agrarian reform for a small place in the sun—for a small plot of land on which to try out the Green Revolution, if you like. In the third place, the population goes on growing and with it the pressure on the land. Finally, a big landowner will not necessarily employ labour-intensive techniques to raise production. In this respect, the high-yielding varieties of seed make no difference in principle.

It may not even be to the big landowner's advantage to maximise production; this, again, is something the Green Revolution by itself cannot change. Professor Michel Cépède, Chairman of the FAO Council, writing in the *International Labour Review* in January 1972, put the position of the large entrepreneur in the form of a rhetorical question: "But why should a plantation owner venture to raise his gross yields, create more jobs and incur higher annual costs in order to secure at best the same return on his investment, particularly his investment in land?" For "he is an entrepreneur seeking to maximise his profits. To him, all forms of cost are the same; the only thing that matters is how high they are. Mechanisation, and especially motorisation, i.e. replacing human labour by consuming a non-renewable asset such as petrol (even if it is liable to be wasted), seems more economic to him than the 'peasant' method of job creation. Operating in a market economy, his aim is not to create the maximum number of livelihoods but merely to sell at a profit."

Professor Cépède concluded that the Green Revolution could indeed increase rural employment, especially as it spreads the work more evenly through the year. By raising farmers' incomes, it should also strengthen the demand for consumer goods produced by village industry. But, he said, "there will be no lasting Green Revolution unless it is carried out by peasants who, because their livelihood lies in working for themselves instead of profiting from the labour of others, have an incentive to farm more and more intensively. [. . .] In other words, land reform, far from being incompatible with the Green Revolution, is essential to its continuation."

A LONG AND COSTLY PROCESS

It would appear, then, that when everything has been done to update the farmer's knowledge and technical resources the need to open up more land to relieve the mounting population pressure cannot be escaped. In areas where suitable land is not available for redistribution, new farmlands can be created only by major pioneering projects to bring the jungle or the desert under the plough. At the very least this entails long and arduous bush-clearing operations—the sort of activity sometimes performed by national youth services—or the building of wells and dams to water the herdsman's cattle on the arid plains.

It is water that brings life to the earth. Thanks largely to the Nile, the average farm in Egypt, which is little more than half a hectare in area, yields the equivalent of farms several times that size in many less favoured countries. It is true that, according to the estimate already quoted, a quarter of the farming population is still redundant on that basis, but the two figures taken together still represent high land productivity and labour absorption. This is illustrated on the national scale in figure 13. More land is now being opened up to the Egyptian farmworker by the Aswan High Dam, yet so rapid is Egypt's rate of population growth that the number of workers requiring employment on the land increased by a greater amount during the years the dam was under construction than the number of new jobs provided by the irrigated acres. This is not to belittle projects of this type, but rather to illustrate the magnitude of the problem.

The cost of employment creation in agriculture on any worth-while scale is generally high, however labour-intensive the methods of reclaiming the land may be. Building a dam by manual labour creates a lot of employment for a time, and that of course is all to the good; but one should not forget that the full cost of the project itself, workers' wages included, is a capital charge on the economy. Not until the reclaimed land is in production is there any pay-off. The great canal of Rajasthan, which the Indian people are building practically with their bare hands across 400 miles of desert, will take 20 years to complete. When its 5,000 miles of feeder canals have been dug, it will turn more than a million hectares of wilderness into arable land and create employment for hundreds of thousands of families; but it is not until the crops have been harvested that the investment will begin to fructify. Granted that new farmland is opened up steadily as the canal advances, the capital outlay still constitutes an impressive act of faith for a country with little to spare. The canal is a gift from the present to the future.

The Colombia mission reported that the cost of expanding agricultural employment by creating new farms was lowest where there was existing farmland which could be procured for redistribution. The Colombian Land Reform Agency assessed the cost per new family farm at 20,000 pesos (about $1,200 at the time) where it was simply a matter of reallocating land already

Population and labour

Figure 13. Agricultural output per hectare and per male worker (world average = 100)

Agricultural output is based on the FAO index of agricultural production (average of the five years 1962-66). The number of active males in agriculture is based on census data of 1960, 1961 or 1962.

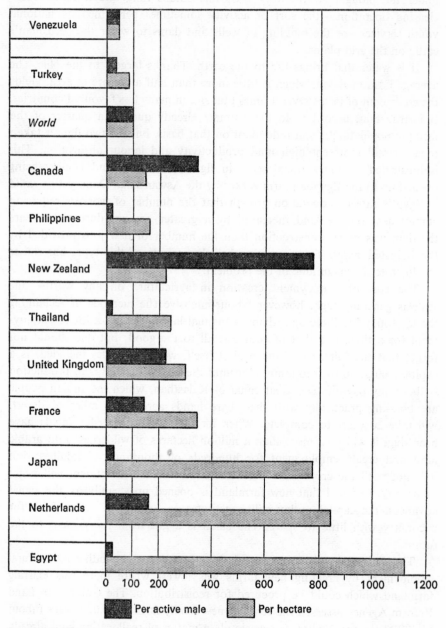

Source: FAO: *The state of food and agriculture, 1968* (Rome, 1968).

being farmed. The cost of settling families on previously unoccupied land in remote areas, on the other hand, was 40,000 pesos per family farm and that of opening up farmland by irrigation was 90,000 pesos per family farm. The 500,000 hectares of new land opened up by the Aswan High Dam cost approximately $1,400 a hectare in terms of capital outlay, but in this case the investment will also earn a dividend from electricity supply. Iraq invested some $250 million of its oil revenues in flood control between 1950 and 1963, and continues to invest large sums in land reclamation—this in a country with a rural population in 1960 of a little more than 4 million and in 1970 of slightly more than 5 million. The cost of opening up 40,000 acres of land by irrigation in Purulia, India, was estimated at 5 million rupees (about $650,000). However one approaches it, creating employment on the land involves a considerable investment of capital (though, in fact, creating industrial jobs requires still more capital).

When all the workers who can be economically accommodated on the land are settled on their new farms or are operating their old farms more efficiently, there will still be a growing rural population in need of work. The Colombia mission's 15-year plan assumed that only half the additional 800,000 jobs required in the rural sector could be found on the farm, notwithstanding an ambitious land redistribution programme which many critics thought politically unattainable, and which the mission itself, as we saw in Chapter 7, realised might be handicapped for many years by shortages of trained manpower. On the other hand, the underemployed village craftsman, who today may be usefully occupied for a dozen hours a week, will benefit directly from the population increase if—but it is a big if—the growing farm community can be gainfully employed. So of course will the economy of the village generally, as the constraint represented by the poverty of the market begins to weaken. None of this, however, can obviate the need for planned rural development, based on small-scale processing and manufacturing industries using local resources. Needless to say, these too represent a substantial aggregate capital outlay, however carefully they are planned to make fullest use of labour-intensive technology.

THE QUALITY OF LIFE

The new generation of villagers in search of employment will be better educated than their parents. We are not concerned in this study with the problem of the so-called "educated unemployed" at the higher level. A situation in which there is a surplus of lawyers and a shortage of agronomists is not a consequence of rapid population growth, but rapid population growth certainly accounts for the increasing numbers of young people who have been to school and are in search of work, assuming, as we surely must, that it is right for children to go to school. The importance of reforming education so that it prepares the young villager better for country life is everywhere recognised, but educational reform cannot make the countryside a better place to live in, nor can it affect the numbers leaving the schools. They will still require employment. And many young people may still feel that work on the family farm or in a small village factory makes too light a demand on their abilities and education, or that the village fails to offer them the values of modern life.

Hence a much bigger investment than that required simply for direct employment creation is urgently called for in the countryside. Houses, hospitals, schools, recreational facilities, water supplies, all-weather roads, transport services—not least to allow outings to the towns—as well as many other features of a modern environment are still woefully lacking in many country districts in the developing world. While the extension of these services will itself employ many workers, the cost implies a heavy investment of capital on which there can be little to show in the way of immediate economic return. Yet if the countryside is to retain even a proportion of the young people, to stay on the land and man the new rural industries, this social investment cannot be withheld.

CAPITAL STARVATION

One of the reasons why rural development has been neglected in the past is that the rural economy of a poor country generates little capital. Overcrowded family farms yield little in the way of a surplus for improvement, whether it be invested by the family directly in the farm or entrusted to the government in the form of taxation. By definition, subsistence farmers consume most of what they produce; the little most of them earn from cash crops pays, as a rule, only for a few other simple necessities of existence, if indeed it pays for so much. At the same time, it must be admitted that rural neglect in many countries has been aggravated by a deliberate policy of favouring the towns. Food prices have been kept down to appease the townsman. Farmers have been taxed to subsidise, in effect, industrial development at the expense of the land. Hence the vicious circle inherent in the rural situation, of poverty making for neglect and neglect consolidating poverty, has been compounded by exploitation. A vigorous infusion of capital from outside the rural environment now seems to be essential if the circle is to be broken. This may imply some foreign aid, but it also suggests that in many countries a larger proportion of the nation's capital resources should be devoted to the rural areas.

The townsman should not begrudge the villager this consideration, because the maintenance of full employment in the towns depends in the end on a prosperous rural market for urban industry, especially in countries where the majority of the people live off the land. When the subsistence farm has practically disappeared and the farmer has some spare cash in his pocket, the town worker's chances of regular employment will be greatly improved. It is the old problem of turning human need into economic demand. There are many manufactured goods the countryman needs, but he cannot at present produce enough to pay for them.

Rural employment, in its turn, depends to a high degree on the prosperity of the town. There is ample evidence that an increase in family incomes in developing countries leads to a bigger demand for food, such is the poverty in which most of their people live. The difficulty again is to translate the huge potential market represented by a growing population into effective economic demand, by creating purchasing power and spreading it as widely as possible. This is an added reason for using the nation's limited resources for paying wages rather than for buying machines, wherever it is feasible to do so. The wages build up a demand of a type which promotes employment and stimulates the growth of a healthy domestic economy. The cost of the machine, on the other hand, may benefit locally only a handful of people who spend much of their incomes on luxury items, very probably imported from abroad, while the majority of the beneficiaries will in most cases actually live in a distant land where the machine was manufactured.

It goes without saying that the increased purchasing power created in this way must be matched by increased production, and that both must surpass the pace of natural population increase if any real progress is to be achieved. This is nowhere more obvious than in the rural areas, where the relationship between hunger and output is only too easy to grasp, especially by the hungry people themselves.

EMPLOYMENT IN THE TOWNS

11

The rate at which the urban population of the Third World is growing has already been indicated. On the United Nations medium fertility assumption, and if the influx from the countryside has been correctly anticipated, the total is expected to advance from 635 million in 1970 to 1,226 million in 1985 and to reach 2,155 million by the end of the century. Thus it will double in 15 years and grow three-and-a-half times in 30 years. About half this urban expansion is expected to come from natural growth, half from the rural exodus. Even so, these figures, as we have seen, conceal the runaway growth of the big cities, which suck in humanity from the smaller towns as well as the country areas. As a consequence, it is not unusual for a metropolitan centre to double its population every ten years.

The degree of urbanisation varies considerably from country to country and from region to region. By the end of the century 43 per cent of the population of the less developed regions as a whole is expected to be in the towns, yet regional variations range from 12 per cent in eastern Africa, through 34 per cent in southern Asia and 40 per cent in western Africa, to 76 per cent in Latin America. These differences reflect mainly the present level of the urban population. In fact the lower the figure, the faster is, often, the pace of migration—for instance, as we saw in an earlier chapter, one of the fastest-growing cities in the world is Nairobi, an eastern African metropolis.

As regards urban employment, it should not be overlooked that, even if by some miracle jobs could be found for those who are already in the towns, this by itself would almost certainly lead to an increased influx from the rural areas. It is for this reason that some people maintain that urban unemployment problems can never be fully resolved until rural birth rates have declined. They point out that as the prospects of work in the town improve, more and more villagers will set out for the city, even though the level of employment there may still be far from high. Hence the dilemma of the urban authorities is that the more they do to alleviate the squalor of the migrant's existence, and particularly if this is effected by improved employment opportunities, the higher the flood of migrants will rise.

Most big cities in the world have a sizeable population of newcomers who have not yet secured employment. In the richer countries they are mostly dispersed through different quarters of the city, where they live relatively inconspicuously in passable comfort. Often they have savings on which to live while seeking employment, and for the majority the time that elapses before they are absorbed into the workforce is generally not excessive. In addition, they may be able to benefit from more or less generous social security services. At best, they represent a necessary link in the never-ending process of replenishing the city's human resources. In the poorer countries, on the other hand, they crowd into slums and shanty towns in direst poverty and may wait years before getting a job, if indeed they ever obtain regular employment. Their expectations are so modest that a slight improvement in the prospects of employment brings additional thousands from the country-side to swell their ranks. In these circumstances the harassed authorities may well ask themselves at times whether there can ever be a solution to the urban employment problem, so long as the population itself continues to grow at anything approaching its present rate.

TOWARDS A STABLE WORKFORCE

At one time the migrant from the fields retained strong links with his home village for many years after moving into the town—usually, in fact, for the rest of his life. When times grew too hard, he would return to the land for a while, to work on the family farm or to undertake casual employment during the harvest. It was his form of unemployment insurance. On the edge of the town, too, there would generally be areas of undeveloped land that were in transition between town and country. Here the migrant and his family might be able to scratch some sort of subsistence during the indigent years. In many parts of the Third World these safeguards against total destitution can still be found, but the sheer weight of the population in need of help renders them increasingly ineffectual. To seek refuge from the poverty of the town in the poverty of the village is for many a worker little better than choosing whether to starve in the streets or go hungry in the fields. At the same time the consolidation of the towns, combined with rural land hunger reaching right up to the outskirts, reduces the opportunities for the family to grow its own food while living, without wages, in a shack on the edge of the city.

The very idea of a town was unknown in many developing countries until recent times. At the beginning of the twentieth century Nairobi was a camp on an empty plain, the temporary quarters of workers building what was then known as the Uganda Railway, with a few small buildings housing colonial officials. By the year 2000 it will have a population of several millions. For a long time the town worker was never fully committed to urban life. He moved backwards and forwards between the town and his village, where he retained his roots. In the town he changed jobs at will, earning a little, spending a little, going home to the village from time to time to help the family with cash and labour, returning to the town when he wanted wage employment again. As recently as 1966 Professor Gutkind found that unskilled workers in Lagos might change their jobs up to eight times before settling into a more or less regular occupation, but he noted that the fear of unemployment was curtailing this mobility.

Many sociologists have argued that a modern economy cannot develop on secure foundations without the evolution of a stable industrial labour force wholly committed to an urban culture, with its roots in the town and the mental attitudes and institutions appropriate to a life style very different from that of the traditional tribal society. The extent to which such a labour force has developed at present varies greatly in different communities. The influence of rapid population growth in this connection appears to be doubly harmful. It compels the all-but-destitute worker to stay in the town, there being no longer much point in commuting to the village, at the same time as it denies him the regular employment which would encourage him to integrate fully into an urban society. With thousands of newcomers endlessly joining the migrant population, the result is a twilight world in which traditional standards tend to disintegrate, with nothing positive to take their place. At best, this leads to a kind of outcast society; at worst, to crime and violence. With populations growing at a more manageable pace, and with the better chances of regular employment which would be one of the consequences, the evolution of a stable, forward-looking urban society would doubtless be greatly eased.

A GRIM OUTLOOK

As things are, the employment prospect in the towns is black indeed. On present trends there could be more unemployed than employed in many of the cities of the Third World within 20 years. The Colombia mission calculated that half the urban labour force of that country might be workless by 1985 if rural migration, natural population growth and employment creation continued at the 1970 levels. Even on optimistic assumptions of greatly increased foreign aid and favourable trends in the terms of trade, the mission still estimated that one worker in three in the urban areas would be without a job within 15 years, unless something radical had been done to turn the tide. The figure today is already one in four. Beyond 1985, the situation would worsen at an accelerating rate if no fall in fertility had begun in the 1970s.

In Kenya it is estimated that out of approximately 650,000 young men and women who will leave school during the 1970-74 Plan period, barely one in ten will find urban employment, although the ambition of the majority may well be to live in a town. It was estimated in 1967 that, in Africa generally, already between 10 and 20 per cent of the population of the larger towns such as Brazzaville, Kinshasa, Accra, Ibadan, Lagos, Abidjan, Nairobi and Dar es Salaam were either totally unemployed or subsisted on very casual employment, and this is quite likely to be an underestimate as the facts are hard to establish in communities growing as fast as these.

The Colombia mission recommended that the invasion from the countryside be held back by a massive policy of rural development, but it recognised that this at best could reduce but not stem the migrant stream. If the mission's proposals bear fruit, out of 5 million additional jobs required between 1970 and 1985, considerably more than 4 million will still be needed outside agriculture, most of them in the towns. The proposals, in fact, call for a 30 per cent increase in agricultural employment and a 64 per cent increase in other sectors. More than 3 million non-agricultural jobs will be required simply to offset population growth; the rest are needed to absorb the existing unemployed. For its part, the mission to Sri Lanka concluded that 1.7 million of the 2.6 million extra jobs required in that country between 1968 and 1983 would have to be created outside agriculture, notwithstanding the fact that an ambitious rural development programme is also urged. The retreat from the land accounts for approximately 1.5 million of the extra workers in need of non-agricultural employment in Colombia through the 15-year period and for approximately 1 million in Sri Lanka. These are fairly typical proportions for developing countries.

THE COST OF JOB CREATION

Normally, it is more costly to create industrial than agricultural employment. The principal constraint on the latter is the availability of land, and on the former the supply of capital. A farm for a family of six, providing two to three workers with full-time employment, can be created in Sri Lanka for the equivalent of about $3,500 by colonising new land, while in Colombia a similar farm employing three or four workers can be colonised for about $2,400. Where large estates are available for distribution, the cost is lower. The average cost of creating one new job in all sectors taken together in Sri

Lanka, on the other hand, works out at about $3,000. In Colombia the cost of creating a new job in the modern manufacturing sector between 1962 and 1966 averaged $14,000 per worker at 1958 prices.

In these circumstances a country having meagre capital resources and a growing army of unemployed workers will usually prefer to invest in the land so long as there is any land to be developed and a market can be found for the produce. Thereafter it will look very closely at the capital cost of creating employment in other sectors of the economy. Unfortunately, capital productivity has been shown to be almost invariably lower in the less developed countries, for despite the chronic shortage of capital much of the costly equipment installed has often been inadequately utilised. The Colombia mission found, for example, that restrictions on shift work and night work compelled management in modern factories to employ expensive machinery below maximum capacity. The estimated utilisation of productive capacity in West Pakistan in 1965 was 37.5 per cent for chemicals, 42.5 per cent for basic metals, 40.7 per cent for electrical machinery and 18.7 per cent for paper and paper products (the United States and Western European levels range from 85 per cent to 90 per cent). This is partly the result of inexperienced management and partly the effect of installing elaborate equipment in the belief that by so doing rapid economic progress is assured, a belief which led in many countries to all sorts of fiscal and importation concessions encouraging the purchase of labour-saving machinery. This tendency was strengthened in many cases by the conditions on which foreign aid was granted by nations sincerely willing to help but also having an interest in the market for capital equipment. Apart from other constraints, the recipient countries did not always have the higher-level manpower needed to make best use of the more modern techniques. Incidentally, it is often the medium-sized enterprises that are the most efficient. The 1960 Census of Industrial Production in Egypt, for example, showed that in 17 out of 20 branches of industry the output per unit of capital was markedly higher in enterprises employing between 10 and 49 workers than in those with 500 or more.

These conclusions only reinforce the case for better utilisation of capital in countries with none to spare. The problem is to employ the greatest possible number of workers while attaining satisfactory levels of production, acceptable quality and reasonable incomes for the workers. The mission to Sri Lanka was not much impressed by the performance of small workshops in that country, but it felt that they could be improved with training and a modest infusion of capital. On the other hand, the Colombia mission assigned a leading employment role to handicrafts and small-scale industry, in a country which is at a more advanced stage of development than Sri Lanka. In India, many years before the World Employment Programme was launched, the encouragement of small enterprises and in particular the handloom industry in order to maintain employment has been a feature of successive Five-Year Plans. The Indian handloom industry employed 3 million workers in 1967, and its share of total cloth production rose from 30 per cent in 1960 to 44 per cent in 1967. By that year handloom production in India exceeded 3,000 million metres of cotton cloth per annum, or more than one-and-a-half times the total output of the British cotton industry. Village industries provided full- or part-time employment to 875,000 Indian workers in 1966, an increase at little capital cost of more than 300,000 in five years.

The choice between capital-intensive and labour-intensive techniques is not always an easy one. A detailed study of alternative techniques for building a 480-kilometre road in a subtropical African country, executed by J. Müller and published in the *International Labour Review* in April 1970, produced an estimated cost per kilometre of $550 using labour-intensive methods and $500 with capital-intensive methods, but the former created 12 times as much employment as the latter. The construction time was the same. What, in such circumstances, should be the decision of a government with limited investment resources?

The cost of creating a job in the service sector naturally varies greatly. It is high in medicine, for example, and relatively low in such activities as small shopkeeping, laundering, the running of modest bars and restaurants. One must also distinguish between communal services such as education and possibly health, and services for which the client pays cash at the time they are rendered. On the former the capital can never be recovered, except through taxation; on the latter it is not only a lesser sum to begin with, but is continuously reconstituted in the normal course of business.

The small bars, restaurants, shops and hand laundries are obviously useful elements in the economy, inasmuch as they evidently provide services wanted by the community; indeed, the encouragement of viable small family businesses of all descriptions can be a way of easing the demand for wage employment in the towns. This is a question, again, of the influence of population pressure on the nature of employment. As with the need to encourage labour-intensive industries wherever there is a reasonable choice, its effect is to modify the structure of the economy.

INDUSTRIAL GROWTH STULTIFIED

The structure of the economy is affected also by the pattern of consumer demand, where large families living close to the subsistence line represent the bulk of the market. Such families spend most of their income on food and the barest essentials, having little to spare for purchases which would stimulate a more dynamic industrial sector. In *Population programmes and economic and social development*, a report published by the Organisation for Economic Co-operation and Development (OECD) in 1970, T. K. Ruprecht and C. Wahren studied the effects of different fertility rates on the structure of the market in developing countries, and through that on the structure of the economy. The report reached the conclusion that rapid population growth did not maximise market size nor yield an optimum market structure, whereas a slowing of the population growth rate produced a more developed economic structure in that the agricultural sector was relatively smaller and the industrial and transportation and communications sectors relatively larger.

For the purpose of the study the economy was divided into five sectors: agriculture, mining, industry, transport and communications, and other services. The initial characteristics were those of a typical developing country. A sustained and a declining rate of population growth rate were then assumed and combined in turn with two different rates of economic growth (3.5 per cent per annum and 6 per cent per annum). The results were calculated at 10-year intervals, up to a point 30 years after the hypothetical decline in fertility began. At the end of that period, with economic output expanding at the 3.5 per cent annual rate, the industrial sector had grown 10.8 per cent more with declining fertility than with constant fertility, transport and communications had grown 7.9 per cent more and agriculture had grown 13.3 per cent less. The figures produced on the 6 per cent economic growth assumption were practically the same. All five sectors had of course grown in absolute terms; the purpose of the study was to show in what way the balance between the sectors was affected by population growth. The authors observed: "The argument that larger populations are desirable as a means of increasing the market is inadequate since it neglects the very important per capita income dimension . . .". The report thus appears to establish clearly the stultifying effect of rapid population growth on industrial development.

POPULATION AND WORKERS' EARNINGS

12

By far the most important requirement for the well-being of a worker's family is a regular living wage or its equivalent in farm income. A solution to the employment problem would have a more direct impact on the workers' standard of living and material security than could any conceivable reform of the social services, quite apart from the indirect benefits flowing through the economy. With full employment the burden on the public welfare services would fall, and at the same time the government's resources for financing them would, in all probability, increase. If it be true that excessive population growth leads to mass unemployment and widespread underemployment, then the most baneful effect of high fertility on workers' welfare is simply the low family incomes that result from shortage of work.

There is no conclusive evidence that rapid population growth actually impedes the expansion of a country's national income. (The national income is the national product plus or minus any foreign earnings or payments.) It cannot be denied that the annual rate of economic growth in the Third World has been much the same over the past decade as in the industrialised nations, while within the Third World itself the highest fertility countries have not consistently done any better or worse than the others. The question is whether they could have attained the same or a faster rate of economic development with a population growing at a slower pace. If so, then average personal incomes today would be higher.

There are opposing views on this question, but most of the experts agree that rapid population growth does in fact tend to retard the growth of incomes per head in countries with little, if any, productive capacity standing idle (other than labour) and without the means of expanding farmland and capital resources at a much faster pace. There is so much underemployment on the land, for example, that common sense suggests that much the same agricultural output could have been obtained with a smaller workforce, especially in countries where the great majority of farmworkers are employed on family holdings. What land is to the farmworker, capital is to the city worker. Hence, on the assumption that the supply of new farmland and of capital resources would not have grown at a rate that was significantly lower with reduced fertility, if it was lower at all, it is reasonable to conclude that the gross national product of most developing countries would have grown at least as fast with slower population growth. Taking a longer view, many experts go as far as to maintain that the rate of capital formation, on which the pace of economic development ultimately depends, is held back in the high fertility areas. The reasons for this were summarised in Chapter 9. If the opinion of these experts is correct, then the total national output could eventually be higher with lower fertility, and the effect on incomes per head would be doubly favourable: not only fewer people to share the cake, but a bigger cake as well.

SOME RECENT ESTIMATES

Until the Third World can save more from its own production it will continue to rely on international assistance for a considerable amount of its development resources. One of the targets of the Second Development Decade is a 3.5 per cent annual growth in income per head, and the Tempo study previously mentioned calculated just what this would entail, in terms of capital investment, at different fertility rates. The authors then compared the results with the probable formation of domestic capital on the same fertility assumptions. The shortfall represented the external aid required. They found that after 15 years of declining fertility the dependence on foreign capital had almost ceased; but with high fertility it was still more than $430 million a year, or the equivalent of approximately 11 per cent of the country's national product. Granted that these are hypothetical calculations about a hypothetical country, they still command respect as an indication of the very strong influence of population growth on capital formation and on the need for foreign aid.

Incidentally, the Tempo study did not confirm the hypothesis that total output would actually rise with lower fertility; throughout the period of the projections, national production rises in the Tempo projections at approximately the same rate on the different assumptions. In each case there is more capital per worker with the smaller population, but the effect of this is offset in the bigger population by the larger workforce. The same national income, however, is shared by fewer people. Other authorities have estimated that in India the advantage of falling fertility would be 3 per cent on the average income after 10 years, between 13 and 16 per cent after 20 years and between 38 and 48 per cent after 30 years. Calculations made independently for Nicaragua, Pakistan and the Philippines produced similar figures. Once again, it is the long-term advantages of falling fertility that are brought out by these models.

Professor Ansley J. Coale has made forecasts showing the effects of reduced fertility on average incomes for periods up to the next 150 years. Coale took as his bases the economic and demographic characteristics of two countries, India and Mexico. He calculated the effect of a 50 per cent reduction in fertility, this being achieved gradually over the first 25 years of his projections, with no change thereafter (note that this reduction would still leave a population growth rate of about 1.8 per cent per annum in Mexico and nearly 1.4 per cent in India, both much higher rates than those of any country in the more developed parts of the world). The formula took into account the improved productivity that was expected to be achieved with the aid of the capital diverted from demographic investment. In other words Coale accepted the proposition that a lower fertility rate leads to a higher rate of capital formation. The exercise is described in *The population dilemma*, edited by Philip M. Hauser.

Professor Coale found that the effects on average incomes of halving fertility were the same in both countries, although the basic data were in many ways quite different. The influence is slow to be felt but accelerates rapidly. Ten years after fertility began to decline, incomes per head would be 3 per cent higher; after 30 years they would be 41 per cent higher, and after 60 years they would be more than double. After 100 years they would be more than three times higher, and after 150 years the income per head would be six times the amount it would have been with unchanged fertility.

He then took the analysis a stage further by calculating what the advantage of a fertility decline that began immediately would be over a decline starting in 30 years time. He illustrated this by showing, decade by decade, the income per head on the first assumption as a percentage of the income per head on the second, "delayed" assumption (see figure 14). During the first 30 years the original assumption (A) naturally makes all the running, though the effect is marginal in the early years. Thereafter fertility on the second assumption (B) begins to decline, but here too the immediate impact is light, and the gap widens. After 60 years incomes are still 50 per cent higher on the first assumption; they eventually settle down, after about 80 years (when the fertility decline will be complete in both examples), at a level about 40 per cent higher. This difference is maintained for the rest of the projection. Thus, if Coale is right, the effect of delaying the onset of a fertility decline for 30 years will still be felt 150 years from now, in the form of average incomes very much lower than might otherwise have been the case. Of course, such

Figure 14.   Projected incomes per head over a period of 150 years

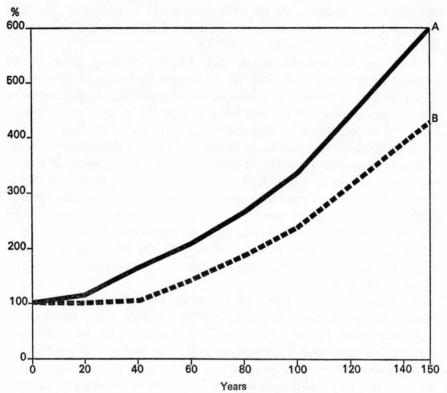

Source: based on Ansley J. Coale: "Population and economic development", in The American Assembly: *The population dilemma*, edited by Philip M. Hauser (Englewood Cliffs, NJ, Prentice-Hall, 1963).

very precise computations may well be upset by time, but there seems to be no good reason to question the general magnitude of the equation. Coale chose a time lag of 30 years, incidentally, because that is the period after which it is thought that a decline in fertility might set in by itself, without the stimulus of official encouragement.

If we take the less favourable assumption that a developing country with lower fertility might achieve merely the same economic output, we can obtain an indication of the effect of population growth on incomes per head by calculating what these would have been in a particular country if the population had grown through a given period at some hypothetical lower rate. The highest demographic growth rate recorded in Europe was 1.4 per cent in Germany in the last decade of the last century. In Britain when Malthus was writing his gloomy masterpiece a century earlier, it was 1.2 per cent. The present annual growth rate for Europe as a whole is little more than 0.75 per cent. Let us take 1 per cent, then, as our hypothetical lower fertility

Table 6. Hypothetical income per head on the basis of a 1 per cent fertility rate

Country	Population (millions)			Income per head	
	Actual 1958	Actual 1968	Hypothetical 1968	Actual 1968 $	Hypo-thetical 1968 $
Chile	7.28	9.35	8.04	449	523
India	412	524	455	71	82
Kenya	7.86	9.22	8.68	119	126
Mexico	33.55	47.11	37.06	513	652
Senegal	3.00	3.40	3.72	182	204
Syria	3.96	5.78	4.37	212	281
Thailand	24.80	34.20	27.39	135	169
United Kingdom	52.10	54.60	57.50	1 469	1 395

Source: Calculated from statistics in United Nations: *Yearbook of national accounts statistics* and idem: *Demographic yearbook.*

rate and see what difference this would have made to incomes per head in a number of typical countries over a ten-year period corresponding roughly with the First United Nations Development Decade, on the assumption that total economic growth was not affected one way or the other.

Table 6 gives the results of this exercise. It will be seen that in the case of the United Kingdom an annual population growth rate of 1 per cent would in fact have reduced average incomes, because the growth of population in that country was only about 0.5 per cent a year. In every other case the income per head would have been substantially higher, after only ten years at the hypothetical rate. It is, of course, not suggested that any of the developing countries listed could in practice reduce its growth rate to 1 per cent in the immediate future. The table is simply a way of comparing what actually happened to average incomes, in countries with growth rates ranging from about 2.5 per cent to 3.5 per cent, with what could have been the result with a lower rate of population growth (which even so would still have been significantly higher than that of most European countries and of the United States). The hypothetical 1 per cent annual population growth rate would have been approximately the same as that of Canada and the USSR.

MORE CONSUMERS, FEWER PRODUCERS

Actual incomes per head for a number of countries are listed in Annex I, as are also the dependency ratios. The dependency ratio (that is, the number of persons aged under 15 and over 65 for every 100 persons between those ages—see also Chapter 13) shows clearly the effect of high fertility in communities where life expectancy is relatively short. Such countries have few older dependants, and the demand for old-age pensions, for example, therefore tends to be low; but this is more than counterbalanced by the fact that they have an ever-increasing number of the population below working age. The effect of different fertility rates on the numbers of dependants, both young and old, is shown clearly by a comparison of the population pyramids reproduced in figure 5.

The population structure forecast for Chile made by Professor Herrick is particularly interesting because it shows the effect of different fertility rates in the same country. Starting with a ratio of 72 children for every 100 adults in the Chilean labour force in 1960, Herrick showed that with unchanged fertility this ratio could be expected to rise to about 74 in 1980 and to 78 by the end of the century, whereas on his lower fertility assumption the ratio would be 51 in 1980 and only 37 in the year 2000. To obtain the full dependency ratio, the numbers of old people would of course also have to be taken into account. At the beginning of the period they would be relatively few, but by the end of the century the effect of improved life expectancy would begin to show. None the less, the calculations are revealing.

At present several countries have dependency ratios around the 100 mark, indicating that the community contains as many dependants as persons of working age. This is usually the sign of a high birth rate combined with a relatively low life expectancy. In such conditions there are few dependants above working age, but on the other hand the working population itself is depleted by early deaths. The countries with such high dependency ratios include Algeria, Kenya, Madagascar; the Dominican Republic, Ecuador, Honduras, Nicaragua; and Iran, Iraq, Jordan and Syria. These are all countries with a crude birth rate above the 50 mark. Only two (Madagascar and Iraq) have a population growing at significantly less than 3 per cent per annum.

At the opposite end of the scale, countries with low birth rates normally have much healthier dependency ratios, notwithstanding the burden of old age. Examples are: Hungary, 52; Italy, 52; Sweden, 51; and Japan, 45. These are all countries with an annual population growth rate well below 1 per cent, with the interesting exception of Japan. In that country birth rates declined so rapidly after the Second World War that today the population aged 15 to 64 (that is, the part of the total population that reflects the earlier fertility pattern) is large relative to the child population. In the Third World it would be difficult to find a country with a dependency ratio below 75. On the United Nations medium fertility assumption, in the year 1980 the average would be 77 for the less developed regions and 57 for the more developed regions. In southern Asia it would be 83; in Africa, 87, in Latin

Huerto Escola

COLABORACION DEL
MINISTERIO DE EDUCACION
CARE
MINISTERIO DE FOMENTO

America, 85. The developing countries' average is brought down by the figure for China, which is put at about 69.

EXTRA MOUTHS AT THE TABLE

At the family level the effect of high fertility on personal consumption is too obvious to need elaborating. Every additional child is an extra dependant, unless indeed the older children can be put out to work. It is in fact the attempt to improve what might be called the "family dependency ratio" that frequently accounts for child labour. When commenting on the high drop-out rate in village schools in an analysis of prevocational training problems in India, Meher C. Nanavatty of the Indian Department of Social Welfare observed that, after the age of 9 or 10, the child becomes an economic asset because he can work and earn something to supplement the family income.

Such a worker may seem to be an economic asset to the family, but child labour obviously can add nothing to the national economy in a country with millions of unemployed, any one of whom could probably do the work of six children. The fact that, none the less, the parents feel compelled to put their children on the labour market is a bitter testimony to the influence of high fertility at the family table. Often it is the arrival of yet another baby which obliges the 9-year-old to go out into the world, to help to win his brother's bread.

Not that the bread is very plentiful. Household income and expenditure surveys bring out clearly the significant fact that poor families spend most of their wages on food. For example, in the rural areas of India in 1957-58 food accounted for 70 per cent of family expenditure. In the cities 62 per cent of family expenditure went on food, but this somewhat lower outgoing was partly the result of families in the towns being obliged to spend more on rent. In Jamaica at the same period household expenditure on food both in the smaller towns and in the country accounted for 60 per cent of the whole. In Mauritius in 1961-62 food absorbed 58 per cent of household expenditure in the rural areas and 49 per cent in the towns, where rents were again substantially heavier. In Morocco in 1959-60 food took over 76 per cent of the household income in the country and over 70 per cent in the town.

Figures for rural households are not always available, but food expenditure would normally be relatively higher than in the towns. In Pakistan in 1955-56 the proportion of the urban wage earner's income spent on food ranged from 56 per cent in Karachi to 75 per cent in Chittagong. In the two principal towns of Tanzania (Dar es Salaam and Tanga) between 1956 and

1958 the percentages were 65 and 68 respectively. Industrial wage earners in Argentina in 1960 paid 59 per cent of their incomes for food; in the four main towns of Colombia in 1952-54 they paid from 48 per cent to 54 per cent, and in Santiago de Chile in 1956-57 they paid 56 per cent. In the two main centres of Indonesia they paid 64 per cent. They paid 52 per cent in 1956 in the capital of the Ivory Coast, and in four of the principal towns of Nigeria in 1959-60 they paid from 49 per cent in Lagos to 58 per cent in Ibadan.

These figures may be compared with 39 per cent for Belgian wage earners, 37 per cent for unskilled wage earners in Denmark, 33 per cent for wage earners in Switzerland and 27 per cent for unskilled workers in the United States. Incomes are of course higher in more advanced countries, but families are smaller also. All these figures are taken from the ILO's *Household income and expenditure statistics, No. 1*, published in 1967. A new edition of this document is currently in preparation, but the general picture will not have changed.

FUTURE FOOD REQUIREMENTS

Notwithstanding the heavy household expenditure on food in the high fertility countries, it is a well known fact that millions of people in those countries have insufficient to eat, and millions who may be able to obtain enough bulk suffer from protein and vitamin deficiency. The statistics have been quoted so often—some of them will be found in Chapter 2—that there is no need to dwell on them here. The Food and Agriculture Organization, in its *Indicative World Plan for Agricultural Development*, published in 1969, showed that if population growth were to continue at its present rate an 80 per cent increase in world food production would be required between 1962 and 1985, simply to maintain present standards. If incomes per head rose at a rate considered reasonable by economists, thus leading to an increase in food consumption per person, the expected rise in the demand for food would be 142 per cent. This would entail an average annual increase in food production of 3.9 per cent, while the trend in developing countries in recent years has been 2.7 per cent.

In Asia and the Far East the total increase in food production between 1962 and 1985 required to provide a reasonable diet is estimated in the *Indicative World Plan* at 154 per cent (that is, more than two-and-a-half times the 1962 output), of which 78 per cent would be required to offset population growth and 76 per cent to meet the heavier demand resulting from higher incomes. With a little more to spend, the assumption is that every family would lay out 43 per cent more on food per person than in 1962. In other words, even after spending the barest minimum on other items, the average household in that region is still able to afford only about 70 per cent of the food it needs. Such are the statistics of indigence.

The food required per individual obviously cannot be influenced by different fertility rates, except to a minor extent through the changed age structure of the population. With reduced fertility, however, there would be fewer individuals to feed. On the United Nations medium fertility assumption, in 1985 there would be about 7 per cent fewer people in the less developed regions of the world than on the constant fertility assumption used by the FAO for its calculations. On the United Nations low fertility assumption the gain would be about 14 per cent. On the other hand, the United Nations Population Division's revised projections show that the previous calculations underestimated probable population growth, largely because death rates have been falling more rapidly than expected. The case for attempting to reduce fertility is strengthened, if anything, by this discovery.

The effect of the Green Revolution on this situation has been much discussed. In the first place, the increasing use of high-yielding varieties of seed could presumably satisfy the world's needs for cereals, if not other foods, at a relatively early date (the lower the rate of population growth, the earlier the date), provided that the wants of the people are translated into economic demand. Another beneficial effect could be in taking up the slack of rural underemployment. However, in discussing the impact of the revolution on landworkers' incomes in Asia in an *International Labour Review* article in January 1972, Mrs. Z. M. Ahmad pointed to some serious drawbacks of the revolution, stating: "Generally speaking, small cultivators, share-croppers and landless agricultural labourers have not benefited from the revolution; regional inequalities and income disparities have been accentuated; there is a widespread fear and danger of labour displacement as a consequence of mechanisation; large and medium-sized landowners have resorted to wholesale eviction of tenants and share-croppers, while those who continue to have their land cultivated by tenants insist on higher rentals. With the introduction of high-yielding varieties of seed there has been an upsurge in the purchase of agricultural land by 'gentlemen farmers', comprising in India and Pakistan, particularly, ex-servicemen, retired civil servants and urban-based businessmen, who have taken up farming as a business proposition and because the discovery of high-yielding varieties makes investment in agriculture profitable. Another attraction for businessmen lies in the generous taxation concessions granted in respect of agricultural ventures. The increase in the investment value of agricultural land has meant that land is gradually being priced out of the reach of small, subsistence or semi-subsistence farmers. The Green Revolution appears to be benefiting primarily those farmers who are already engaged in commercial production rather than subsistence farmers and, among the commercial farmers, the big ones more than the small producers." Clearly, some of the hopes of the Green Revolution are still far from being realised.

FULL EMPLOYMENT VERSUS WAGES

In the wage-earning sector, it should not be forgotten that workers' incomes are directly influenced by the discipline of employment planning, imposed in part at least as a consequence of population growth. Labour-intensive industry spreads the work, but capital-intensive industry pays the rates. In present circumstances it is obviously more important to spread employment than to pay high wages to a small minority operating modern equipment. Spreading the work also has the advantage of spreading purchasing power and so creating the healthier consumer market on which, finally, fuller employment depends. None the less, a high wage economy has never yet been achieved without a relatively capital-intensive technology. All the studies demonstrating the competitive character of labour-intensive techniques in developing countries indeed assume that labour will be relatively cheap.

One of the aims of development planning is, of course, to build up the amount of capital per worker, so as to attain the higher productivity without which better incomes cannot be earned, but meanwhile it appears that full employment can only be sustained by a low wage economy. Since this policy of spreading the work is forced upon developing countries to a considerable degree by population pressure, and since, as we have noted, high fertility tends to inhibit capital formation, demographic factors are evidently retarding the process by which a high wage economy is created.

Economists are in broad agreement that economic prosperity in the modern world begins when no more than about 30 per cent of a nation's workers are still employed on the land. In France the farm population in fact constitutes 15 per cent of the total, while in New Zealand it constitutes 13 per cent. Professor K. C. Abercrombie, in an analysis published in the FAO *Monthly Bulletin of Agricultural Economics and Statistics* in April 1969, pointed out that according to the FAO's *Indicative World Plan for Agricultural Development*, although the number of persons engaged in agriculture is increasing greatly, the percentage of the total population that these people represent is expected to decline from 65 per cent in 1962 to 53 per cent in 1985. Hence the number of non-farm families for every farm family should rise between 1962 and 1985 from 0.54 to 0.91. Abercrombie calculated that, even after allowing for the increased demand for food needed to redress present privation, this expansion in the domestic market would permit an average annual increase in incomes per head from agriculture in the develop-

Figure 15. Number of persons below the $100 a year poverty line at different fertility rates (calculated for a typical developing country starting with a population of 10 million)

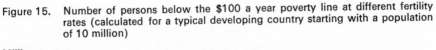
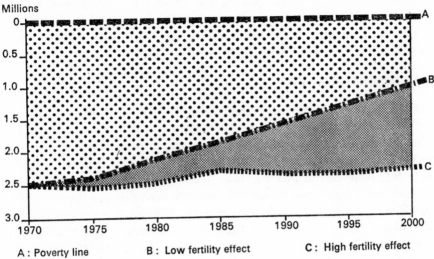

A : Poverty line   B : Low fertility effect   C : High fertility effect

Source: Tempo (General Electric Center for Advanced Studies), *Economic benefits of slowing population growth*, 1971.

ing countries of only about 2 per cent. He concluded that because rapid population growth slows down the rate at which the occupational structure of the population can be changed, it retards the improvement of agricultural incomes and levels of living.

It seems, then, that the economic planners who went for intensive industrial investment were not as naïve as they may now appear. What frustrated their designs was that they could not create the industrial openings quickly enough to accommodate a labour force that was expanding too rapidly. As a consequence, developing countries are now compelled to encourage workers to stay on the land by every means that can be devised without being actually repressive, while conceding that this is not finally the road either to rural prosperity or to rapid economic progress.

Incomes per head have risen steadily in the Third World over the past two decades. It would be churlish to belittle the achievement, and untrue to claim that they had failed to keep pace with population growth. What has disappointed governments, eager in their new-minted freedom to lead their people out of the darkness of poverty, is that progress has seemed bitterly slow. Average incomes have risen, but they would almost certainly have risen faster if birth rates had been lower. As for the future, the Tempo study calculated that, after 15 years of declining fertility, incomes per head would be 11 per cent higher than with unchanged fertility. Starting with an income per head of $200 in 1970, the projections produced a figure for 1985 of $225 with unchanged fertility and one of $284 with reduced fertility. For the end of the century the figures were $352 and $478 respectively, a difference of 36 per cent. The effect of different fertility rates on the number of people below the $100 poverty line is shown in figure 15.

INCOME DISTRIBUTION

Finally, it should not be forgotten that the term "average income" conceals the effects of unequal distribution. There is a crying need for research into the relationship between population growth and income distribution in the developing countries. Who in fact has received the increased income? It is difficult to believe that a growing family living off the same small plot of land has in every case managed to increase production to the extent suggested by the statistics on average incomes. Millions of such families, frequently comprising a majority of the population, must be sinking every year deeper into poverty, even where they own their own farms. If they are not owner-occupiers, the imposition of higher rents—or actual dispossession—often deepens the inequality, in the absence of effective protection from the law. The urban worker, too, must in many cases be worse off than before, despite the higher wages of some of his fellow townsmen.

THE SQUEEZE ON SOCIAL SECURITY 13

In addition to his own earnings, the worker and his family enjoy such social benefits as the community can afford. The combined value of these to the average family has sometimes been called their "social wage". By adding this sum to the breadwinner's earnings, after deducting taxation and any direct contribution that he himself may be required to make to the social services, an impression can be obtained of the "true" wages the worker is drawing from the economy. In countries with highly developed community services the social wage can come to a substantial sum. In less favoured societies, for obvious reasons, the social wage is small. Poor to begin with, high fertility countries are also compelled to devote such a large proportion of their resources to a single service—education—that the others tend to be starved.

The need for different social security cash benefits—for instance, family, maternity, invalidity, survivors' and unemployment benefits—will clearly vary with the demographic structure of the community and with the pace at which families are growing. The question is whether rapid population growth, in general, helps or hinders the development of an adequate social security system covering the whole of the population. There is also the reverse consideration: do social security benefits influence population growth? All social benefits, obviously, transfer part of the family burden from the parents to the State. Hence many of the disadvantages of high fertility, which are easy enough to demonstrate in most countries in terms of the national economy and the state budget, are not immediately felt by the family man, who may indeed believe that he profits from having a large number of children when welfare benefits are generous.

SOCIAL SECURITY AND THE BIRTH RATE

Governments wishing to stimulate population growth often endeavour to do so by paying ample children's allowances and by putting other social

125

advantages in the way of the large family. France is perhaps one of the best-known cases in point. Other, more densely populated countries are caught between the desire to provide their people with a high standard of social security and the national advantages of keeping population growth at a low level. Despite government attitudes, however, there is not much evidence to show whether social security payments have, in practice, any positive influence on family size in countries such as these. It is difficult to picture a couple calculating the financial balance of having or not having another child and agreeing that the scale is tipped by the extra francs or pounds that might be expected from the public purse, still less deciding to have two or three more offspring in order to boost the family income. The effect is probably more of a passive character. The knowledge that the government favours larger families and that a useful part of the cost of rearing a child will be borne by the State may tend to make married couples rather more casual in their attitude to birth prevention. Even so, there seems to be no clear correlation between birth rates and the level of social security benefits in countries at comparable stages of social progress.

Only a rich society can pay high social benefits. In such a society average wages will generally be high, and so will the cost of bringing up a child; hence the effect of the children's allowances will still be relatively marginal in most families. Similarly, a country in which workers' incomes are barely above the subsistence level will itself, generally, be too poor to offer anything but the slenderest social benefits, if indeed it can provide any cash benefits at all. In most developing countries the great majority of the workers are outside the wage-earning sector and as a rule are therefore beyond the scope of the social payments system. Thus in both societies there would appear to be a natural regulator preventing social security payments from having a powerful direct influence on fertility.

In the richer societies there is certainly little evidence to show that generous social security benefits encourage fertility. Figures published by the ILO, for example, indicate that in the mid-1960s average social security expenditure for all purposes was the equivalent of $304 per person per year in Sweden, $290 in the Federal Republic of Germany, $258 in France, $242 in New Zealand, $237 in Luxembourg, $215 in Belgium, $210 in Canada, $202 in Norway, $201 in Denmark, $197 in the United States and $195 in the United Kingdom, to name only the "top ten" where the figure was around the $200 mark or higher. The nation at the head of the list has one of the lowest birth rates in the world—14.3 per 1,000 of the population in 1968. More recent figures, published in December 1971 by the French Institute of Demographic Studies, revealed that fertility had fallen below reproduction level in seven countries, of which three (Denmark, Federal Republic of Germany, Sweden) are in the above list.

FAMILY ALLOWANCES

If an attempt is made to isolate the effect on fertility of child allowances as such, the picture appears to be, if anything, even less revealing. The overall figures given above are in several cases mainly accounted for by pensions and public health service costs. They conceal very wide differences in the payment of family allowances, which range from 4 per cent of all social security payments in the Federal Republic of Germany to 31 per cent in France. In France in 1963, in fact, family allowances accounted for more than 4 per cent of the total national income, whereas in the Federal Republic of Germany in the same year they absorbed barely 0.5 per cent; in Switzerland, where all social payments averaged $157 per head, they accounted for less than 0.1 per cent of the national income. In other words these payments, expressed as a percentage of the national income, were eight times higher in France than in the Federal Republic of Germany and more than 40 times higher than in Switzerland, yet the annual birth rate in each of these three countries is approximately the same, at about 17 per 1,000 of the population. The countries which paid the highest proportion of their national incomes in child allowances, after France, were Belgium (3.01 per cent), Austria (2.89 per cent), New Zealand (2.58 per cent), Czechoslovakia (2.57 per cent), Italy (2.53 per cent), Luxembourg (2.41 per cent), the Netherlands (2.24 per cent) and Chile (2.24 per cent), to name the countries out of the remaining 34 in the list where the figure exceeded 2 per cent. The annual birth rates per 1,000 of the population in these countries are respectively 15, 17, 23, 15, 17, 14, 19 and 35. It is difficult to discern any pattern here.

In France the birth rate rose after the war years but eventually began to decline again, being marginally lower in 1968 than that of Austria, the Federal Republic of Germany, the Netherlands, Norway and the United Kingdom, all of which are countries which make no attempt to stimulate population growth and in some cases tend to discourage it. It is as yet too early to say whether the French Government's more recent measures to reverse this trend have been successful. In the absence of much more extensive research, therefore, the question must be left open, with a strong presumption that family allowances have, if anything, only a minimal effect on fertility in relatively affluent societies.

It is difficult to dissect the motives of a man and woman embarking on parenthood. The results of a sample survey of white married women in South Africa suggested that slightly larger families might result "if adequate family allowances were made available", but what the different persons questioned would consider "adequate" and what the effect would be in practice nobody can say.

It can be argued that family allowances are more likely to encourage population growth in really poor families, especially where the family is poor but the community is relatively rich. In such circumstances the welfare benefits might seem attractive to the penurious parents, who conceivably might see in them an inducement to child-bearing. One hears of individual instances where this is said to be the case, but the evidence is seldom reliable. In developing countries, where the nation as a whole is poor, the situation is different. For the reasons already mentioned, family allowances are bound to be meagre, if they exist at all, and in any case touch only a small part of the population. A report prepared for the Population Commission of the United Nations in 1969 named 63 countries which were operating family allowance schemes in 1967. The list included 20 African countries (not counting South Africa) and half a dozen in Latin America, with Asia represented only by Iran, Israel, the Khmer Republic, Lebanon, the Republic of Viet-Nam and the Democratic Republic of Viet-Nam.

An interesting feature of the list is that all the African countries are French-speaking and all but Israel in the Asian group were formerly in the French sphere of influence. This is a striking example of the persistence of culture. It is true that the African countries include Zaire: but Zaire was formerly the Belgian Congo, and, as we have seen, Belgium is second only to France in its promotion of family allowances. In nearly all these African countries the dissemination of birth control literature is forbidden by law. Hence it might be expected that high fertility would be doubly encouraged—positively by the provision of family allowances and negatively by official hostility to contraception. Yet the birth rate in these countries is in general no higher and in several cases distinctly lower than in English- and Arabic-speaking African countries where both factors are often reversed: no family allowances, no opposition to birth control. Thus Algeria, Ghana, Kenya, Morocco, Nigeria and the Sudan all have birth rates above the average for the continent. Of this group, only Algeria and Morocco operate family allowance programmes. To discover why one African country has a higher birth rate than another is beyond the scope of this survey. A number of extremely complex relationships—ethnological, cultural, educational, economic, possibly even political—would require scrutiny. The point is that family allowances do not appear to be a major determinant, at any rate given their present scope.

There are, of course, sometimes abnormal situations. France's generous attitude to family support, for example, assumes that monogamous unions are the normal rule. Where high fertility is combined with polygamy, however, the claims that a husband may make on the social security services can be extraordinary. A sample survey, conducted when child allowances were being paid out at the offices of an African benefit fund, discovered one beneficiary, a commercial employee with normal monthly earnings no higher than 6,000 francs, who drew 69,300 francs in family and other benefits for the third quarter of 1966, plus 196,700 francs in back payment for the previous two quarters. He had 8 wives and 32 children. (The francs would be West African or Central African francs worth about one-fiftieth of a new French franc.) Another beneficiary, a hospital worker, drew 50,300 francs for the one quarter. He has 12 wives and 30 children.

One of the effects of family allowances in such cases is undoubtedly that they enable the worker to support a large number of wives. If he were deprived of financial support from the social security fund, he might practise a sort of family limitation by taking fewer consorts. Since 1 man with 12 wives normally means there must be 11 men without a wife, this would appear to be socially more just, but it would not necessarily reduce the birth rate. In the first case quoted, the average wife had four children and in the second between two and three. In a monogamous society, or in a polygamous society where men's incomes were more evenly distributed, the total number of births could be just as high. It might well be higher, as there would be fewer young women married to older husbands. Some countries have met the difficulty of sustaining a family allowances scheme in partly polygamous societies by placing a limit on the number of children for whom a father may claim. In Iraq the limit is three, in Morocco six, in Togo six and in Tunisia four.

The recipients of family allowances are a highly privileged minority in the Third World. Statistics compiled for Africa in the early and middle 1960s show, for example, that children qualifying for family allowances made up 7 per cent of the appropriate child population in the Central African Republic, 3 per cent in Chad, 5 per cent in Dahomey, 13 per cent in Gabon, 4 per cent in Madagascar and 13 per cent in Senegal. When we consider that most of the workers in these countries are outside the wage economy, these percentages are by no means derisory, but they do indicate the limited possibilities. We must remember, too, that in the majority of countries of the Third World the percentage is zero. One of the effects of rapid population growth in such societies is simply to postpone the introduction of children's allowances to a far distant date, inasmuch as it hampers the development of a modern economy with a predominantly wage-earning labour force. Meanwhile, most developing countries would probably not put family allowances high in the list of social security priorities. Given their scant resources, medical care and provisions for old age would probably have stronger claims.

MATERNITY BENEFIT

The other welfare payment immediately affected by high fertility is maternity benefit, defined in the ILO Social Security (Minimum Standards) Convention, 1952, as payment for "pregnancy and confinement [. . .] and sus-

pension of earnings [. . .] resulting therefrom". France and 14 African countries formerly administered by France provide prenatal allowances for the
whole of the nine months preceding childbirth. While the majority of women
in the 14 African countries will not be covered because of their being outside
the wage economy, these are still the only States in the world recognising
the mother's right to an allowance throughout the period of pregnancy.
Another 67 countries, making 82 in all, had maternity insurance programmes
of one sort or another in 1967, including 55 in the developing world. This
meant that 23 developing countries which felt they were not in a position
to introduce family allowances were none the less endeavouring to do something
for the working mother on the occasion of childbirth. Thus there is evidently
widespread agreement that the family should be assisted at this time.

The very little that most developing countries can do in practice again
reflects a situation where meagre resources are confronted by enormous
demand. The birth rate in the less developed regions of the world, as we
have seen, averages about 40 per 1,000 and in the more developed regions
18 per 1,000. Hence, other things being equal, the world's poorest countries
would have to pay more than twice as many maternity allowances as the
richest, in proportion to their populations. Conversely, the potential gains
from reduced fertility are of the same order. A country like India, where
between 25 and 30 million births occur every year, would have to cope with
only about 10 million if it had the same birth rate as Europe. And that is
not the most extreme case. Burma, Dahomey, Ecuador, Ghana, Iraq, Kenya,
Nicaragua, Nigeria and the Sudan, to name but nine countries, have three
times and in some cases nearly four times the number of confinements in
countries like Poland and Sweden, relative to their populations. There cannot
be a simpler example of the influence of rapid population growth on the
need for social security.

As with family allowances, some countries see maternity benefits as an
incentive to population growth. The ready provision made by France and
by countries following the French example are evidently part of a general
system favouring the large family. In Bulgaria, the German Democratic
Republic, Luxembourg and the USSR maternity payments increase as the
family grows. In Spain, in addition to the normal maternity allowances,
a national award of 5,000 pesetas is made every year to the married couple
with the largest number of children, with smaller prizes in the provinces.
It is not suggested that couples will have more and more babies in the hope
of winning a medal; the effect is rather to make fecundity famous, and so
encourage the notion that a big family is something to be celebrated.

Elsewhere the trend is in the opposite direction. Nine former French
African colonies abolished birth grants during the 1960s, apparently feeling

that the regular monthly maternity allowances were enough. In some countries maternity allowances are reduced as the family grows, and in others they are cut off altogether. In January 1968 two Indian state Governments (Mysore and Uttar Pradesh) ruled that the paid maternity leave enjoyed by state employees should in future be limited to the first three confinements, and their example was followed later that year by a third state, Maharashtra. About the same time the Government of Malaysia introduced a similar amendment for its employees, terminated the practice of relating salaries to the number of dependants and raised the age at which couples could obtain housing grants. All four governments justified what by itself was undeniably a retrograde step by pleading the overriding national claims of lower fertility.

The United Nations Advisory Mission to India in 1965 recommended that "such incentives to childbearing" as maternity allowances "should if possible be removed". However, the Indian Government's Committee on Labour Welfare, which reported in 1969, held that curtailing maternity benefits as a means of discouraging conception could be misunderstood. That this might be so is suggested by the headline under which the *New York Times* reported the restrictions on maternity benefits for state employees in Maharashtra in September 1968: "Indian state to penalise parents who exceed quota of three children". If the sub-editors of one of the world's best-informed newspapers saw it that way, a mother expecting her fourth child in Bombay might be excused for feeling she was to be punished for having a baby.

The difficulty here was in taking away a benefit that had previously been enjoyed. Most authorities appear to share the feeling of the Indian Government that maternity benefits, once introduced, are too important to mother and child to be abolished. On the other hand, it can be argued that where parents are given every facility for family limitation, and when they also know exactly on what terms maternity benefits may or may not be claimed, they embark upon another pregnancy with their eyes open. Where the parents are well enough off to have another child without privation, there is clearly some sense in this argument. The restrictions mentioned above in Mysore, Uttar Pradesh, Maharashtra and Malaysia applied to employees of the state, whose earnings and security of employment are presumably better than the average in those areas. Many countries limit the number of children on which income tax rebates can be claimed, and there is not, as a rule, a feeling that this is socially unjust. In India itself tax concessions are limited to the first two children.

THE REAL CONSTRAINT

Whatever one's views on this controversial question, it is significant that the value of such an obviously desirable welfare benefit as a maternity allowance should be questioned by many sincere and well-meaning persons because of the need to curb population growth. In practice, the constraint on the provision of this and other social security payments, however, in most parts of the Third World is poverty, not policy. As a general rule, only wage workers benefit from these provisions and in some developing countries only government employees do so.

This limitation is imposed inevitably by the low average income in high fertility countries at an early stage of development. There are broadly four ways in which social security may be financed: (1) the worker's employer may be made directly responsible for meeting the cost, in which event he will normally try to insure against at least part of the liability; (2) an insurance fund may be created from compulsory contributions by workers and employers, or by employers alone; (3) a provident fund may be constituted in the same way, this being really a form of compulsory saving, with the worker receiving only the sum contributed in his name; (4) the system can be financed from general taxation. In practice, countries with well developed social security schemes adopt a combination of methods, according to the contingency and persons to be covered. It will be seen that only the fourth method, general taxation, can readily be used to benefit workers outside the wage-earning sector in a comprehensive manner.

The self-employed are brought into the compulsory national insurance system in several industrialised countries where, however, they constitute a minority of the population which, if necessary, can be subsidised by the State. Where the self-employed are the vast majority and are living near the poverty line, the task of collecting their contributions would generally be uneconomic, even if they could afford to pay them. In such circumstances some of the workers might be able to do something for themselves through their own organisations (such as co-operative societies), but there is little the law can do except to encourage the formation of such institutions. Hence in countries where taxation possibilities are severely limited, the extension of social security payments to the mass of the population is likely to be a very slow process. For obvious reasons, rapid population growth aggravates this situation.

HELPING THE WORKLESS

Unemployment benefit is of course restricted to wage earners even in affluent societies, for the reason that a self-employed person cannot be said to dismiss himself or recruit himself. In developing countries, in addition to this inherent limitation, the provision of unemployment benefit is handicapped by severe operational and financial difficulties. Unemployment insurance schemes can work effectively only where labour is recruited through employment exchanges at which the unemployed are registered. The assumption, in fact, must be that the labour force is restricted, more or less, to insured workers and that their periods of unemployment will be on average of moderate duration. In developing countries suffering from widespread unemployment and, moreover, with the available labour growing all the time through rural migration as well as through natural increase, these conditions can rarely be met. Employment offices, where they exist, tend to be bypassed, and the insured worker quickly runs out of the modest benefit to which his previous contributions have entitled him. As a consequence of these difficulties unemployment insurance even in an embryonic form is hardly known in the Third World. A recent survey revealed that only four developing countries in Latin America, two in Asia and one in Africa provided some form of unemployment benefit. So long as the problem of unemployment, exacerbated as it is by population pressure, remains intractable, it is unlikely that this situation can be radically changed.

Meanwhile, it should be noted that what the self-employed farmer needs in order to provide income security is security of land tenure, with a guaranteed market and guaranteed prices for his produce. This is his equivalent of unemployment insurance, if that is defined broadly as the assurance of a minimum livelihood so long as he is willing and able to work. If his produce is mainly for the home market, the average farmer's income, in countries where a majority of the labour force works on the land, is unlikely to rise much above subsistence level, for the reasons given in the last chapter. The countries whose farmers enjoy relatively high guaranteed prices are those where non-agricultural workers constitute the mass of the population and are at the same time comparatively well paid, or where the produce is for export to other well-to-do nations for whom agricultural imports are a necessity. In either case the farmer is producing for a strong market, a situation in which it is possible to negotiate the necessary guarantees. This is not generally the position with developing countries.

Where a country's principal crops are for export, income security calls for international agreement. The United Nations Conference on Trade and Development has been attempting for many years to secure more favourable terms for the Third World in this respect, but the reaction of the consumer nations, by and large, has been disappointing. "These issues, so hard fought in international conferences," observed the ILO Colombia mission, "need to be considered anew in the light of the growing crisis of unemployment."

Rapid population growth may not make it more difficult to reach satisfactory international commodity agreements, but it certainly makes it more urgent to do so. Population pressure may also mean that, however fair the price, the resulting income has to be shared by too many hands to provide an adequate livelihood. There is no way of relieving the want of the under-employed farmworker, doing his stint on a family plot too small to occupy fully all the adult members, in the many developing countries where they are the rule rather than the exception. Only employment creation can alleviate this brand of poverty, or indeed most other brands of poverty. The best form of income security, after all, is job security. So long as mass unemployment and underemployment are rampant, there will be little the State can do to relieve the concomitant poverty, whether by price supports for the farmer or by unemployment benefits for the wage earner.

SECURITY IN OLD AGE

Old-age pensions are in a category of their own. They provide for the only contingency normally covered by social security legislation which every adult is certain to experience if he lives long enough, and which will not end so long as life lasts. Traditionally, the children supported the parents in old age, and this is still the most common form of retirement insurance in the world, clearly recognised as such by both children and parents.

In Western society, before the State assumed some responsibility for old age, certain major employers such as the railways, the police, the army and the civil service introduced modest retirement pensions for their workers. This is broadly the position now reached in many developing countries. To qualify for such a pension one often has to work the greater part of a lifetime with the same employer. A recent analysis of statutory pension insurance schemes in countries publishing official statistics on the subject revealed that nowhere, apparently, in the Third World was more than a small minority of the workers protected. In the mid-1960s the proportion of the labour force covered by pension insurance was 17 per cent in Costa Rica, 14 per cent in Ecuador, 3 per cent in Mali, 16 per cent in Mexico, 6 per cent in Morocco, 26 per cent in Panama, 13 per cent in the Philippines and 5 per cent in the Syrian Arab Republic. These figures are quoted in *Poverty and minimum living standards*, published by the ILO in 1970.

Several governments of developing countries are now attempting to assist the elderly out of general taxation, even where the provision of other social security benefits is minimal. The Bahamas and several Indian state governments, for example, have made a start with modest retirement pensions which benefit the retired landworker and self-employed artisan as

well as other members of the community. Rapid population growth affects the provision of such pensions in two ways. Firstly, the tremendous strain placed on the available resources by the ever-growing expenditure on children's welfare cruelly handicaps provision for the elderly. Secondly, the population structure is such that old people represent only a small fraction of the whole. The expectation of life in most developing countries is still so short that few live into the mellow years. If the normal retirement age for both sexes is taken as 65, the average African dies 20 years before the retirement age, the average Asian does so 15 years before, and the average Latin American 5 to 10 years before. These figures are based on the average life expectancy at birth. A person who survives to working age will normally live longer than this average, but his chances of reaching retirement are still lower than in more advanced societies. According to figures given in the United Nations *Demographic yearbook*, the average male aged 15 in Ghana, for example, may expect to reach the age of 54, in India 56, in Colombia 59, in Egypt and Mexico 67 and in Sri Lanka 69. These figures may be compared with France 70, Canada 71, the United Kingdom 72, Denmark 72, Norway 73, the Netherlands 73. A margin of only one or two years in the life expectancy of the average worker can make a significant difference to the cost of retirement benefits, given that, in the two most favourable instances just cited, the average pensioner draws his benefit for only eight years. There might be no great difference in the life expectancy of persons who actually reached retiring age, but the numbers doing so would be smaller in the one case than in the other.

Another indication of adult mortality trends can be obtained by comparing the number of persons in a given age-group with those who survive into the age-group above. Thus in Africa in 1960 there were 18.25 million persons aged 45 to 54. Ten years later the population aged 55 to 64 (i.e. the same individuals) totalled 14.57 million; hence 3.68 million, or 20 per cent, of those approaching retiring age had died during the decade. A similar calculation produces figures of 17 per cent for Asia, 14 per cent for Latin America and only 6 per cent for Western Europe. These conclusions ignore the effect of intercontinental migration, but the significance of this would be negligible.

PENSIONS AND EMPLOYMENT

One worker in 30 in the world today would be in retirement if a pension were provided at 65. If, in the less developed regions, their countries are unable to assist them, this is partly a consequence of the huge expenditure necessitated by high birth rates.

Several authorities have suggested that the provision of old-age pensions might, by reducing the dependency of the aged on their children, remove the need for large families felt by many parents in the Third World. At the same time it would help to create employment for younger workers. Thus Goran Ohlin observed that, in the poorest countries, old-age pension schemes seem far away, since much public spending is done for the sake of child welfare and education, where it relieves the private dependency burden and possibly weakens the economic deterrent against large families. He found that in principle there is a strong case for spending some at the narrow top of the age pyramid where it might have the opposite effect. The ILO mission to Sri Lanka proposed that a small pension should be paid to all persons over 60 who were unable to find support, and that the existing provident schemes should be extended to a greater number of workers, as a relatively inexpensive means of removing older persons from the labour market. Where this is one of the objects it is essential, of course, that the payment be conditional on cessation of work; in other words that there should be a clear distinction between retirement benefit and old-age benefit in the strict sense of the term. In many countries this distinction is firmly drawn; in others, the pension can be claimed at the appropriate age in any event.

A BURDEN FOR THE FUTURE

As life expectancy improves in the Third World, more of the population will reach retirement age. If present trends continue, most of the children now living in developing countries will qualify, some day well into the next century, for whatever old-age pensions their countries can provide. Thus high fertility combined with falling mortality is building up this load for future generations. It is true that, at the same time, the labour force will have expanded for the same reasons, so that the ratio of old people to the population of working age will not have changed significantly. This might be of some comfort if one could be sure that all the other difficulties created by high fertility will have been overcome—not least the problems of finding employment for an enormous labour force and of growing the food for young and old alike.

Any reduction in fertility beginning now will obviously have no effect on the size of the aged population for another 65 years. Other things being equal, the absolute total will then be only gradually affected, but meanwhile the relative diminution in the numbers of children and younger workers will be shifting the balance towards the aged. This long-term change is clearly illustrated by the age-structure of countries where birth rates have been relatively low for several decades. It can be seen at a glance in figure 16 and in the population pyramids reproduced in figure 5, as well as in table 7. The number of old persons relative to the population of working age in the United

Figure 16. The dependency load (based on 1970 population)

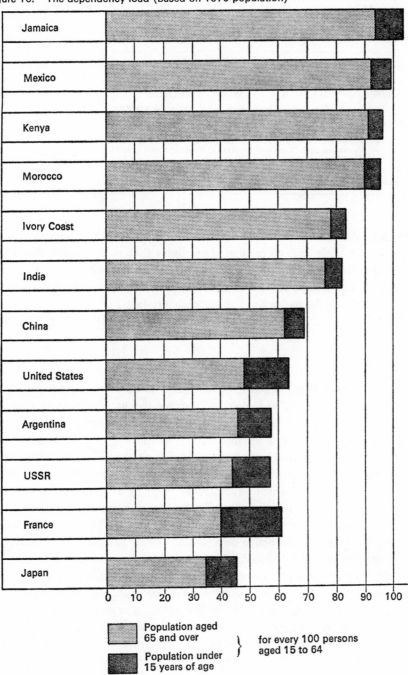

Source: based on United Nations Population Division statistics.

Table 7. Dependency load per 1,000 persons aged 15 to 64 : some typical figures from 1970

Country	A	B	C	Country	A	B	C
Brazil	771	64	835	Morocco	895	51	946
Ethiopia	750	55	805	New Zealand	541	140	681
Finland	377	134	511	Sri Lanka	715	68	783
Ivory Coast	775	50	825	Syrian Arab Rep.	908	62	970
Martinique	799	90	889	United Kingdom	380	222	602

Key: A = Population under 15 years of age for every 1,000 persons aged 15 to 64.
B = Population aged 65 and over for every 1,000 persons aged 15 to 64.
C = Total load.
See also Annex I.
Source: based on United Nations statistics.

Kingdom, for example, is more than four times that of the African countries listed in the table and more than three times that of the Asian and Latin American countries, excepting only Martinique. Countries such as the United Kingdom have to find large sums for old-age pensions, but normally they are able to do so because of the high productivity of the labour force and the fact that the child population is relatively less demanding.

THE DILEMMA

The dilemma facing developing countries is how to expand the social security system without widening still further the gap between workers in the relatively modern sector of the economy and the mass of the people. The position was summed up in a report adopted by the ILO Governing Body in March 1972, from which the following passage is taken: "The initial limitation of the scope of the social security schemes and the principle of extending it gradually, which have been adopted by a number of developing countries, are a wise and realistic policy whenever resources are limited and the infrastructure weak. Any attempt to cover from the beginning the whole of the country and all its active population is likely to lead to administrative chaos or to inapplicable legislation, which would only undermine the authority of the law or of the social security institutions. On the other hand, the principle of gradual extension of social security ordinarily gives an advantage to workers who are better off in the first place as regards job security and level of wages. Accordingly, the ILO's task is twofold: (1) to show, on the one hand, that limited schemes can only be justified as a transitional measure which must be superseded and improved as soon as circumstances permit; and (2) to suggest special protective measures to be adopted in the meantime for the sections of the population, mainly rural or self-employed, likely to remain outside the scope of schemes catering essentially for employees in urban areas". The report continued: "The task is to find in each case what realistically can be done to raise living standards through social security and what is politically, economically and financially acceptable in order gradually to reduce social inequalities in individual countries."

One need hardly add that the execution of this task is rendered immeasurably more difficult by the never-relenting pressure of population. With reduced fertility and the faster rate at which incomes per head might improve in consequence, the day when a given nation might afford an effective system of social security for all its people could be brought perceptibly nearer. At the same time, a steady reduction in the proportion of the labour force working as peasant farmers or self-employed artisans would ease many of the technical difficulties which limit the scope of social security in practice. This change, too, as we have seen, is closely tied up with demographic factors.

THE EXPANSION OF
WELFARE SERVICES

14

It remains only to look at the influence of rapid population growth on the provision of welfare services, as distinct from cash benefits. The chief of these are education, health and housing.

On education, one need only add the point that, of all the welfare services, this is the one where the burden of population growth is transferred most completely from the family to the community. With regard to health, it is obvious that the most serious consequences of high fertility are the ill-effects of overcrowding in insanitary homes, of malnutrition and undernutrition, and in particular the suffering of children and the strain on the mother of frequent childbirth, often when she herself is weak and undernourished. Population pressure also aggravates sanitary deficiencies outside the home, particularly in the overcrowded urban areas, one of the results being a high incidence of communicable diseases.

In these circumstances, improved health requires, above all, measures to improve the environment. The difficulties under which the public health authorities labour in urban communities multiplying at the rates mentioned in Chapter 8 can scarcely be imagined. At the same time, it should not be forgotten that many rural areas lack the most basic conditions of an environmental health policy, such as a pure water supply, drainage, sewage and garbage disposal. The Colombia mission reported, for example, that 54 per cent of the Colombian rural population was without a safe water supply in 1965, compared with 10 per cent in the towns. In this regard, as in others, the rural authorities are faced with the daunting task of repairing past neglect while all the time the population in need of protection is growing. Shortage of funds and above all of qualified personnel at all levels, constrains progress.

MEDICAL CARE

The provision of medical care for the worker and his family is doubly handicapped by population growth. To the extent that population pressure contributes to poor health, it increases the need for these facilities. At the same time, it obviously does so directly by multiplying the number of potential patients. One of the most obvious illustrations is the shortage of qualified midwives. Other things being equal, high fertility countries should clearly have many more midwives than low fertility countries. Cameroon, for instance, has approximately the same population as Switzerland, but the birth rate in the African State is about 50 per 1,000 and in the Swiss Confederation it is 17 per 1,000. There should therefore be approximately three times as many midwives in Cameroon as in Switzerland, to provide a comparable service. In fact, in 1967 there were 76 qualified midwives in Cameroon and 1,760 in Switzerland. To reach the Swiss level in relation to the incidence of maternity cases, Cameroon would have required more than 5,000, or nearly 70 times the actual number. It is true that in African villages there are generally old wives to help with deliveries, but it is the policy of every African government to replace these in time by qualified personnel, who can provide up-to-date prenatal and antenatal care as well as assisting at the confinement.

The figures for Cameroon are fairly typical of the Third World. With a qualified midwife for every 9,000 of the population, Cameroon is in fact better served in this respect than many countries. To give a few less favourable examples, the ratio is 1 to 21,000 in Senegal, 1 to 35,000 in Algeria, 1 to 37,000 in Bolivia, 1 to 51,000 in Sri Lanka, 1 to 86,000 in Morocco, 1 to 148,000 in Afghanistan, 1 to 165,000 in Ecuador, and less than 1 to 200,000 in Nepal. By contrast, there is a qualified midwife for every 2,000 of the population in the United Kingdom in the public health service alone. With a birth rate of 17 per 1,000, this means that the average midwife in such a country looks after 34 confinements each year, in addition to other duties. In a country such as Bolivia, on the other hand, there is a qualified midwife for every 1,600 deliveries. In Morocco the ratio is 1 to 4,300.

If there ought to be three times as many midwives in many developing countries as in low fertility States of the same size, there should also be three times as many maternity hospitals, three times as many prenatal and antenatal clinics, three times as many nurseries, three times the number of gynaecologists, three times the provision of vitamins and nutrients for expectant mothers. Granted that in any case most developing countries would still be a long way behind the wealthier nations in this respect, the fact remains that high fertility doubles or trebles the demand, making it an almost impossible task to attain modern standards in the near future.

In addition to the heavier demand for maternity services in proportion to the population, the high fertility country is also of course rapidly expanding its population. There is therefore a compound effect. If the calculation is made again in the case of Cameroon and Switzerland, the position roughly is that Cameroon today should have three times the maternity services of Switzerland, while in 30 years time it would require five times the services to reach a comparable level, if there is no change in fertility. The farther one peers into the future, the greater the gap becomes.

A fall in fertility, on the other hand, would obviously have a reverse effect. It would reduce, eventually, the number of women having babies, as well as the number of times each woman required maternity care. In a country with the typical characteristics of "Developa", the imaginary State used in the Tempo study, a reduction in the birth rate from 44 per 1,000 to 30 per 1,000 occurring gradually over 15 years would make a difference at the end of that short period of about 250,000 deliveries a year; the calculation is that there would be 698,000 confinements with unchanged fertility and 455,000 at the lower rate. The saving in the demand for maternity services in this instance is thus of the order of 36 per cent. We have already seen in Chapter 12 that incomes per head would be 11 per cent higher in the same circumstances. Thus not only would the demand for welfare services be lower with reduced fertility but the resources to pay for them would be more plentiful. Compared with the constant fertility situation, the amount available per confinement would be about 50 per cent higher after only 15 years of falling fertility, assuming that maternity services continued to claim the same share of the national income.

A CONSTANTLY RISING DEMAND

The demand for other medical services can be expected to rise at least as fast as the rise in population. Kenya, for example, with a population growing by 3.3 per cent every year, would have to expand medical services six or seven times as fast as countries like the United Kingdom and France, with population growth rates of about 0.5 per cent, merely to continue in its present relative position. India would have to maintain a pace nearly three times as rapid as the United States. The task of actually reducing the gap between rich and poor countries in these circumstances is manifestly of Herculean proportions. Yet these comparisons, sobering as they are, still fail to bring out the full measure of the challenge. All medical experts agree that, unless fertility is reduced, developing countries will not only have to meet the needs of an increasing population but must expect a higher incidence of disease than the countries in the more developed regions.

Recent returns show that there was only 1 doctor to approximately 18,000 people in Tanzania, 1 to 27,000 in Zaire, 1 to 31,000 in Nigeria, 1 to 40,000 in Nepal, and 1 to 60,000 in Ethiopia. In most countries in the more developed regions there is a doctor for rather less than every 1,000 people. In the Soviet Union the ratio is 1 to 450 and in the United States 1 to 650. The numbers of hospital beds display a similar contrast; 1 to every 100 people in most parts of Europe and North America, 1 to over 2,000 in Nigeria and Ethiopia. Further figures will be found in Annex I.

It says much for the determination of developing countries that these ratios in most cases are an improvement on those in previous periods, despite all the obstacles to be overcome. One can only regret that so remarkable an achievement should have been cut back by population growth. It is reasonable to assume that governments would have made at least as great a drive to provide health facilities if fertility rates had been lower, and they might well have made bigger advances since much less would have been required for investment in education. In either event they could have closed the gap further with lower fertility. A country with an annual 3 per cent natural growth rate which succeeded in raising the number of hospital beds from 1 per 1,200 to 1 per 1,000 of the population in ten years would have reduced the ratio to 1 to 820, if population growth had been 1 per cent per annum and the same number of additional beds had been provided.

These figures, moreover, conceal the grave inequalities that may exist within the same country. In the rural areas medical services usually fall far short of those in the towns. Past neglect, the scattered nature of the population and the unattractiveness of rural life to many medical and paramedical personnel combine to make it difficult to redress this imbalance, given that both funds and trained manpower are in short supply. The Colombia mission, again, quoted official returns for that country showing that in 1966 there were 10 doctors per 10,000 inhabitants in municipalities having a population of over 100,000, while at the other end of the scale the ratio in municipalities with fewer than 20,000 inhabitants was 0.52 per 10,000. Medical consultations in the rural areas averaged 31 per 1,000 inhabitants annually and in the bigger towns 100 per 1,000. Medical attention during pregnancy was received by 18 per cent of expectant mothers in the rural areas, by 46 per cent in the small towns and by 73 per cent in the major towns. Thus, with population growth increasing the demand both in town and country, it is the rural areas that tend to be left behind.

Where the medical service is provided as part of an employment scheme the gap between town and country, or between wage earner and the self-employed farmer or artisan, inevitably grows even wider. In India doctors in the service of the Employees State Insurance Corporation in 1966 averaged

1 to every 1,000 insured workers, or 1 to every 3,800 persons including the family, while in the nation as a whole the ratio was 1 to every 5,700 persons, and in the rural areas 30,000 inhabitants had to share a doctor between them.

Thus, social progress too often leaves behind the peasant on his farm and the craftsman in his village workshop. In India, as in many similar countries, every person is entitled free of charge to whatever public medical services are available; but the pressure on resources is such that all this means for many rural workers in the Third World is that they are free to make use of something that, as yet, scarcely exists. At the time the above figures were quoted, some 3.5 million workers were insured under the Indian ESI scheme, making with their families about 13 million persons covered out of a total population in that year of just under 500 million. If all the workers covered by other medical insurance schemes in India are added, including about 7 million in government and quasi-government employment and more than 1 million on the railways, the total number of insured Indian workers at the time would have been less than 17 million out of a labour force of about 210 million. The benefits of a welfare service of this type will spread to increasing numbers of the community as the structure of the economy changes: but the structure changes slowly.

HOUSING

Closely bound up with the worker's health is the standard of the accommodation in which he lives. Housing is not yet everywhere recognised as a social service, although it can clearly be seen as a social problem. Landworkers live in squalor for lack of clean water and sanitation, while in the cities millions are scarcely protected from the elements. In both cases high fertility adds daily to the congestion, and those who flee from the fields only compound the degradation of the streets. There is no need to repeat the over-all figures for urban growth given in Chapter 8. Behind the wall of the communal statistics are the homes in which people live. In the three main towns of Ghana in 1960 more than one-third of the people already lived 20 and more to a house, and the situation, far from getting better, was getting worse. In Zaire, according to the 1962 census, nearly nine urban dwellings out of ten were deemed to require major repairs or were so unhealthy that they should have been pulled down. Most of them are still occupied. In India one family in three in the rural areas lives in a single room *or less*, and in the big cities the proportion rises to two families out of three. Nearly one-third of the dwellings in the capital city of the Republic of Korea are shacks occupied by two or three families. In Iraq at the last housing census

145

80 per cent of all dwellings were built of non-durable materials and 64 per cent were considered unsuitable for habitation.

To give these facts is not to pillory the countries named. Like the rest of the Third World, they are caught up in a crisis of housing generated by the endlessly rising demand. If the population of the Third World is going to double between 1970 and the end of the century, which is the median expectation of the United Nations Population Division, then clearly the number of dwellings will also have to double, without making up any of the backlog. In the towns the number of dwellings would have to increase more than three times. In other words, in 30 short years the world's poorest nations need to build the equivalent of three towns for every one standing today: and that would still leave the same numbers living in the slums. Think of any large town, and imagine what that entails.

In an attempt to estimate the demand for housing in the year 2000, the United Nations assumed that by that year 95 per cent of all households in the Third World would have a separate dwelling. If this standard is to be attained, 380 million new dwellings will be required in developing countries to replace existing property, and another 670 million will be needed to accommodate the increased population. Thus, out of every three houses that ought to be built, two are necessitated by population growth.

In the world as a whole an estimated 1,400 million new dwellings will have to be built in the 30 years to provide reasonable housing standards. As a rough indication of what this entails at the community level, it means that one new dwelling should be erected every year for every 100 of the population. A country with a population of 10 million should therefore be building 100,000 new dwellings a year. Very few developing countries approach this rate of construction, which was the target set up by the First United Nations Development Decade. Instead of 10 new houses per 1,000 people each year, the majority of countries in Africa, Asia and Latin America were able to complete an average of only two or three of adequate standard. Returns for 1967 showed that in some countries the figure was as low as 0.5 per 1,000 of the population.

It is hardly necessary to emphasise, once again, that one of the factors accounting for the disappointing performance on this front was population pressure, the endlessly growing demand. To reach the United Nations target, the developing world as a whole would have been required to build 20 million houses in the first year of the Decade, and this figure would have risen to 25 million in the final year. On the same basis, developing countries will have to build 33 million in the last year of the Second Development Decade and 50 million in the year 2000. The effect of a fall in fertility can be deduced from Professor Herrick's projections for Chile. On his high fertility assumption, Chile would have to be constructing about 275,000 new dwellings a year at the end of the century to maintain the rate recommended by the United Nations, while with reduced fertility the target could be lowered to 150,000.

FINANCIAL DIFFICULTIES

It is true that with high fertility there would be more workers to build the houses, and if economic development had continued at a satisfactory pace there would be more capital to pay their wages and to purchase the necessary raw materials. The question once again boils down to the effect of high fertility on capital formation. Since house building can be a highly labour-intensive industry and its raw materials are or can be mostly locally produced, it might appear that this is one sphere in which population growth need not obstruct progress. The difficulty is that the cost of erecting a house to modern standards is still far beyond the means of the families most in need. Even well organised self-help housing projects in which the worker, in effect, builds his own house in his own time, call for a capital outlay for materials and the installation of services which the poorest families cannot contemplate. At the same time, there can be little assurance that the capital would be repaid if grants were made for the purpose from public funds. The rate of house building is largely determined, in the long run, not only by what a nation as an economic entity can save, but even more by what the prospective occupants as individuals can spare for rents or mortgage payments.

It is this which places housing as a welfare service in a category of its own. Houses differ from schools and hospitals in that they are not for communal use; they are occupied by individuals or families. Public funds can therefore normally be earmarked only for loans to families who can afford to repay them over the years, or for building houses for rent. The same limitation applies to building societies and other forms of co-operative housing enterprise. Given that no government or co-operative society in a developing country can contemplate giving houses away free of charge or heavily subsidised at the community's expense, the inevitable consequence is that most housing projects in the poorer parts of the world benefit mainly the wage-earning minority who are in steady employment and the relatively prosperous farmer with a little money to spare. The final constraint on housing is therefore very directly related to incomes per head. The breakthrough will come when these rise above a certain level.

Population growth accentuates the need for housing and at the same time prevents the growth of income. In the Third World, prospects for adequate housing are indeed dim, but this is not to say that nothing can be done in the matter. Enlightened public housing programmes, research and experiment in low-cost house construction, training of building workers to higher standards, legislation to make building land available at a reasonable price, an equitable taxation and public spending policy to ensure that common services such as water and sanitation are provided for as wide a segment of the population as possible, the creation of financial institutions to enable the occupants to pay for houses in the most convenient way, a national housing policy to stimulate the building and improvement of homes for the people to the limit of the available resources—all these measures are currently being taken by progressive administrations in a number of countries as part of a general policy of community development. Where houses are let for profit or provided as a condition of employment, governments can also control rents and impose minimum standards. The essential thing is to make sure that as the worker's income rises he is encouraged and enabled to devote a significant part of his improved earnings to bettering the living accommodation of himself and his family, while the government expands the necessary communal services to meet the demand.

This is not the place to enter into the housing problems of the developing world in any depth. Our purpose is simply to draw attention to the influence of rapid population growth on certain aspects of the workers' lives. With respect to housing, that influence appears to be wholly negative and harmful.

A GLOBAL PROBLEM

It would be possible to extend the discussion of workers' welfare by considering many other things—widow's pensions, the care of orphans, the rehabilitation of the handicapped, recreational and cultural facilities, the growth of free institutions serving the workers' welfare such as co-operative societies and trade unions, and indeed almost everything that might enter into the life of a typical family. The conclusions, however, will be much the same, in principle, as they are for the major factors we have examined in these last three chapters. If it is a fact that population pressure in a particular country obstructs the growth of personal incomes, of social security benefits, of education, medical care and housing, it will in all probability stand in the way of most other forms of social progress. If, on the other hand, rapid population growth can be seen to be stimulating progress in these fields, it is a fair assumption that it also stimulates progress in other branches of social welfare. This question, like all others, finally resolves itself into the basic issue: whether high fertility helps or hinders a nation's development, over whatever period of time a government considers crucial. The correct answer may not be the same in every country of the world.

These are necessarily material standards. There are no statistics by which the happiness of a large family with an adequate income can be compared with that of a small one. Who can say whether parents and children would be more content if the average number of children per marriage was two instead of, say, five? All one can say is that with over-large families it seems only too certain that in many countries children will be hungry, the family will be clothed in rags, the home will be a shed or a hut, sickness and disease will breathe at every door, opportunities for training and employment will be meagre and that the liberating and exhilarating force of education will be held at bay.

When the conquest of poverty is further advanced, a different approach to population might become possible in certain countries, for a time at least. In the world as a whole, it seems only common sense to assume that eventually the population must be stabilised, if the resources of nature are not to be exhausted.

At what point on the demographic curve that day will come no expert is at present able to say. The only sensible conclusion would appear to be that governments and people should face the possibility frankly while there is still time. The crisis of population is not just another of the many problems afflicting developing countries; it is a world crisis. Densely populated Western States may be able to support large populations by reason of their technological brilliance, but in the final analysis they depend for their raw materials and for food itself on the world at large. We live in one world and in this one world, finally, we shall eat or starve together.

ANNEXES

I. SELECTED POPULATION STATISTICS IN 20 COUNTRIES

Country	Population [1] (millions)		Births and deaths per 1,000 persons [2]			Years required for population to double	Average life span (years) [3]
	1970	1985 (est.)	Births	Deaths	Increase		
Developed							
Australia	12.5	17.0	20	9	11	63	71
France	51.1	57.6	17	11	6	116	72
Japan	103	121	19	7	12	58	71
USSR	243	287	17	7	10	70	70
United States	206	253	17	9	8	87	71
Less developed							
Africa							
Egypt	33.9	52.3	45	21	24	29	52
Kenya	10.9	17.9	50	17	33	21	43
Nigeria	55.1	84.7	54	27	27	26	—
Sudan	15.8	26.0	52	19	33	21	40
Zaire	17.4	25.8	43	20	23	30	39
Asia							
China	760	965	40	20	20	35	—
India	555	808	45	18	27	26	41
Indonesia	121	184	45	21	24	29	47
Iran	28.3	45.1	50	19	31	23	—
Turkey	35.6	52.9	40	15	25	28	54
Latin America and the Caribbean							
Argentina	24.3	29.6	23	9	14	50	66
Chile	9.78	13.6	35	12	23	30	52
Colombia	21.4	35.6	44	12	32	22	45
Jamaica	1.99	2.57	33	7	26	27	65
Mexico	50.7	84.4	45	10	35	20	59

[1] United Nations Population Division: *World population prospects 1965-1985*.   [2] Population Council: *Population and family planning: a factbook* (New York, 1971). Based on United Nations: *Population and vital statistics report*, Jan. 1970. Where upper and lower estimates are quoted, an average is given here.   [3] At birth. Latest figure given in United Nations: *Demographic yearbook 1968*. Male and female average.   [4] Attending primary or intermediate school, not necessarily remaining for the whole period. In certain cases figures may be underestimates, caused by

Percentage of children aged 5-14 at school in 1965 [4]		Population in 1967 [5]		Dependency ratio in 1970 [6]		Labour force in 1970 [7]	Income per head in 1968 [8] (US$)
Boys	Girls	per doctor	per hospital bed	A	B		
97	81	850 [9]	80	46	13	41	1 991
71	81	850 [9]	140 [9]	40	21	43	1 927
100	99	920	80	34	11	50	1 122
	81	450	100	44	13	51	—
100	100	650	120	48	15	40	3 578
56	36	2 150	570	79	6	27	156
52	38	10 240	730	91	5	40	119
37	23	31 000	2 310	85	4	41	68 [9]
	13	22 020	1 050	85	5	32	97
73	33	27 030	—	76	6	46	52
	58 [10]	—	—	62	7	46	—
	40 [11]	4 830 [9]	1 670 [12]	76	6	40	71
48 [13]	42 [13]	27 560	1 450 [12]	84	5	34	86
	33 [9]	3 750	960	89	7	27	252
52 [13]	38 [13]	2 760	560	77	7	45	321
71	71	620	160 [12]	46	11	36	609
70	68	2 320	250	71	8	31	449
42	44	2 220	420	93	5	29	299
65	67	1 490	270	93	10	33	411
61	57	1 820	510 [9]	92	7	28	513

differences in national education systems. Unesco: *Statistical yearbook 1968*. [5] WHO: *World health statistics annual 1967*, Vol. III. [6] Based on United Nations population statistics as note [1] above. A = persons aged under 15, B = persons aged 65 and over, as percentage of persons aged 15-64. [7] As percentage of total population. ILO: *Labour force projections 1965-1985*. [8] United Nations: *Yearbook of national accounts statistics 1969*, Vol. I. [9] 1966. [10] 1958. [11] 1963. [12] 1965. [13] 1964.

II. THE WORLD AND ITS PEOPLE : POPULATION GROWTH RATES

Based on latest available estimates. The boundaries do not imply official endorsement or acceptance by the ILO or the United Nations.

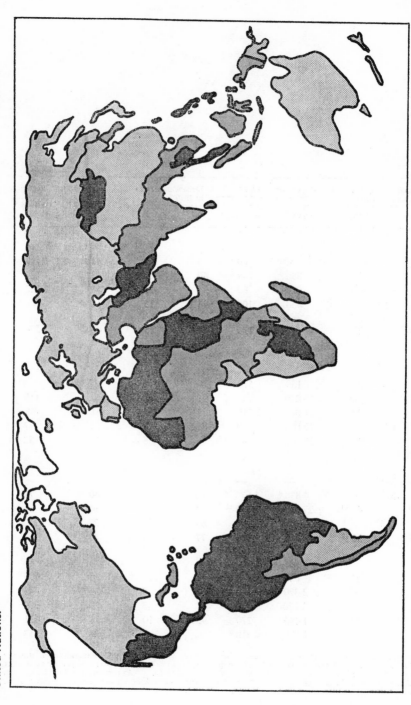

Areas with up to 1 per cent annual population growth

Areas with 1 to 2 per cent annual population growth

Areas with 2 to 3 per cent annual population growth

Areas with over 3 per cent annual population growth

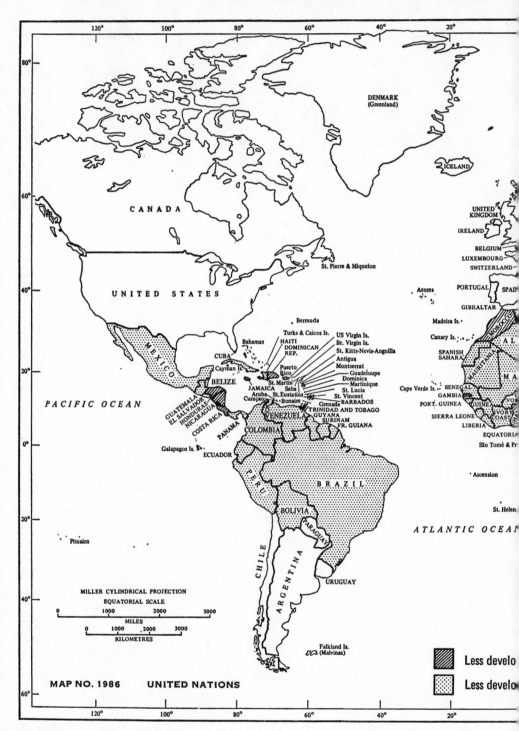

MILLER CYLINDRICAL PROJECTION
EQUATORIAL SCALE

MAP NO. 1986   UNITED NATIONS

Less develo

Less develo

The final status of Jammu and Kashmir has not yet been determined.
Dotted line represents approximately the Cease-Fire Line.

The boundaries shown on this map are not, in some instances, finally
determined and their reproduction does not imply official endorsement or
acceptance by the United Nations.

Country names revised 1973

IV. A NOTE ON ILO POPULATION ACTIVITIES

The International Labour Organisation has been active since its foundation in areas affected by population trends—in employment, migration, human resources development and social security, for example. In recent years, world alarm at the possible consequences of rapid population growth has led to the ILO's direct involvement in the solutions to population problems as such. The ILO has a modest but distinctive contribution to make in view of its tripartite structure and established expertise in work-related social services, with which substantive links can be forged in population matters. In November 1968 the Governing Body of the ILO laid down the following lines of action in support of policies to moderate population growth in developing countries, where appropriate: (1) promotion of information and educational activities on population and family planning questions at various levels, particularly through its workers' education, labour welfare and co-operative and rural institutions programmes; (2) policy-oriented research on the demographic aspects of social policy in certain fields, such as employment and the promotion of social security; and (3) action to stimulate the participation by social security institutions and enterprise-level medical services in the promotion of family planning.

The purpose of the educational action is to create an awareness and understanding of population problems among the ILO's constituents—trade union and management circles, and public authorities responsible for employment and labour policies. In appropriate cases the ILO further provides stimulus and support to the involvement of the institutions concerned in the formulation and implementation of population policy measures within its sphere of competence. These new lines of activities under the enlarged mandate are largely financed by the United Nations Fund for Population Activities.

Population problems are complex and raise sensitive issues. In particular, they vary in nature and severity in various countries and regions. In planning and developing ILO action, full account is taken of these differences in needs, cultural characteristics and political attitudes. The ILO's activities in the field of population, as in other fields, are designed to respond to the needs and wishes of the Organisation's constituents and are planned and imple-

mented with their close collaboration. There can therefore be no question of imposing a single, centralised approach.

There are two main lines of thrust in the ILO activities aimed at education and institutional involvement. The first is oriented towards workers and their organisations and the second towards the employers and their organisations. Regional advisers for the education of the workers in matters of population have been or will be appointed in the various developing regions. A start has been made with the appointment of regional advisers for the orientation of employers in these matters. A number of regional and national seminars, training workshops, and so on, for union leaders, managers, educationists and others have already been organised. This programme is currently being intensified, in association with workers' and employers' organisations. A limited number of training fellowships and study tours are awarded by the ILO to enable selected personnel from management and labour to observe developments in other countries. Since 1972 the International Institute for Labour Studies in Geneva has included a course on population policy in its leadership training programme.

Since its inception the ILO has been directly interested in occupational health and in social security institutions serving workers and their families under industrial insurance and provident schemes. Occupational health and social security medical care facilities can serve, in appropriate cases, as effective channels for the provision of family planning and related welfare services to the insured population. In recent years, advisory missions have been sent on request to several countries for this purpose. Several regional advisers have been appointed to undertake promotional, advisory and training activities. A start is being made with orientation and training courses for occupational health and welfare personnel.

The prospects for these activities of work-related institutions and services are improved where a favourable combination of certain factors exist. These factors include: a firm commitment of the government and the people to population policy; a reasonably large modern sector; an adequate stage of development of the institutions and services of the modern sector; and a good industrial relations climate. Subject to these conditions, the ILO aims to promote, notably in Asia, an intensive programme of family planning and related measures for the benefit of workers employed in the modern sector. Since the workers' families in this sector are to some extent already motivated towards family planning and can be readily reached through organisations and social services, there are good grounds for believing that the spread of family planning practices and a significant reduction in fertility might be achieved reasonably quickly in the case of this limited but key social group. This approach calls for an enlarged concept of labour welfare, which would place family planning services alongside job security, social security, occupational health, and so on, as an essential aspect of workers' welfare.

To encourage this approach, the various ILO regional advisers for population activities in Asia have been grouped to form an Asian labour and population team. Moreover, the ILO organised, in collaboration with the Economic Commission for Asia and the Far East (ECAFE), an Asian symposium on labour and population policy, held in Kuala Lumpur in July-August 1972, which drew up guidelines for translating this approach into practice.

Educational publications include the present volume and a booklet to be published in collaboration with the Asian Trade Union College of the International Confederation of Free Trade Unions, entitled *The Asian worker and the population problem*. A handbook underlining the implications of rapid population growth for employers in developing countries is planned, as is a booklet on family planning in industry, containing selected case studies, to be addressed to employers' and workers' organisations and national authorities responsible for labour questions and family planning programmes. The preparation and supply of training material and audio-visual teaching aids on various aspects of family planning coming within the ILO's jurisdiction is a growing feature of the educational activities of the Organisation.

The ILO has initiated a comprehensive research and action programme on the interaction between population and employment factors under its World Employment Programme. The project is designed to consolidate and enlarge the existing knowledge base in this field and to ensure that population and demographic aspects are more fully taken into account in activities under the World Employment Programme. The major purpose of this research is ultimately to prepare policy and action-oriented studies specific to selected individual countries. The main topics to be studied substantively include the following: the determinants of labour force participation; the economics of fertility, particularly the effects of labour force participation, employment structure and unemployment on fertility; and the effects of population growth on dual socio-economic structure, technological choice and income distribution, and through these variables on the level, growth and structure of employment. This research is being organised in co-operation with a network of research institutions in the various developing regions. It is envisaged that the project will be completed in 1975.

Another important area of research is the interaction between social security and population dynamics. The first phase of this project, which began in 1972, will study the contribution of social security (particularly family benefits) to population policy, especially in regard to family norms and fertility regulation. Field studies are envisaged to determine what differences, if any, result from the various systems of family allowances and what is the effect of the health and social activities of social security institutions on parental attitudes and family size. These inquiries will be conducted in collaboration with national institutions.

The ILO is constantly engaged on the development of comprehensive statistics on the labour force, employment, unemployment and underemployment. It provides expert assistance to governments in connection with problems of measurement, collection, dissemination and analysis of these data. The ILO compiles and publishes statistics from population censuses and from sample surveys on the sex-age structure of the population and of the labour force and on its distribution by industry, occupation and status. The research and analytical activities in this area are designed to elucidate the relationship between these factors and various aspects of economic development and planning, particularly as they relate to problems of employment, unemployment and underemployment. In 1971 five volumes of labour force projections, taken at five-year intervals to 1985, were published, covering every country in the world. A sixth volume (a methodological supplement) was published in 1973. This series will be updated at suitable intervals.

Much of the ILO's work in the population field that is financed by the United Nations Fund for Population Activities is undertaken as the Organisation's contribution to the United Nations worldwide population programme. The Organisation is of course represented on several joint bodies where an inter-agency approach is desirable. An obvious example is the Preparatory Committee for the 1974 World Population Conference.

V. GUIDE TO FURTHER READING

Abercrombie, K. C.: "Population growth and agricultural development", in *Monthly Bulletin of Agricultural Economics and Statistics* (Rome, FAO), Vol. 18, No. 4, April 1969.

Bartsch, W. H., and Richter, L. E.: "An outline of rural manpower assessment and planning in developing countries" (3 parts), in *International Labour Review* (Geneva, ILO), Vol. 103, Nos. 1-3, Jan.-Feb.-Mar. 1971.

Glass, D. V.: "Fertility trends in Europe since the Second World War", in S. J. Behrman, L. Corsa and R. Freedman (eds.): *Fertility and family planning: a world view* (Ann Arbor, University of Michigan Press, 1969).

ILO: *Employment and incomes policies for Iran* (Geneva, 1973).

— *Employment, incomes and equality: a strategy for increasing productive employment in Kenya* (Geneva, 1972).

— *Matching employment opportunities and expectations: a programme of action for Ceylon* (Geneva, 1971), 2 vols.

— *Poverty and minimum living standards: the role of the ILO*, Report of the Director-General/Part 1, International Labour Conference, 54th Session, Geneva, 1970.

— *Social security: a workers' education manual* (Geneva, 1970).

— *The cost of social security 1964-1966* (Geneva, 1972).

— *The World Employment Programme*, Report IV, International Labour Conference, 56th Session, Geneva, 1971.

— *Towards full employment: a programme for Colombia* (Geneva, 1970).

International Planned Parenthood Federation: *Family planning in five continents* (London, 1971).

Johnson, S.: *The population problem* (Newton Abbot, David & Charles, 1973).

Jones, G. G.: "Underutilisation of manpower and demographic trends in Latin America", in *International Labour Review* (Geneva, ILO), Vol. 98, No. 5, Nov. 1968.

Laing, W. A.: *The costs and benefits of family planning* (London, PEP (Political and Economic Planning), 1972).

Lewis, W. A., *et al.:* "Economic research for the World Employment Programme", in *International Labour Review* (Geneva, ILO), Vol. 101, No. 5, May 1970.

Medawar, J., and Pyke, D. (eds.): *Family planning* (Harmondsworth, Penguin Books, 1971).

Morse, D. A.: *The origin and evolution of the ILO and its role in the world community* (New York School of Industrial and Labor Relations, Cornell University; distributed outside the United States by the ILO).

Myrdal, G.: *The challenge of world poverty: a world anti-poverty programme in outline* (New York, Pantheon Books, 1970; Harmondsworth, Penguin Books, 1971).

National Academy of Sciences: *Rapid population growth: consequences and policy implications* (Baltimore, Johns Hopkins Press, 1971).

Nortman, D.: *Population and family planning programs: a factbook,* Reports on population and family planning (New York, Population Council, 1972).

Ohlin, G.: *Population control and economic development* (Paris, OECD Development Centre, 1967).

Ominde, S. H., and Ejiogu, C. N.: *Population growth and economic development in Africa* (London, Heinemann (in association with the Population Council, New York), 1972).

Oppenheimer, V. K.: *Population*, Headline series, No. 206 (New York, Foreign Policy Association, 1971).

Paukert, F.: "The distribution of gains from economic development" in *International Labour Review* (Geneva, ILO), Vol. 91, No. 5, May 1965.

Prebisch, R.: *Change and development: Latin America's great task* (New York, Praeger, 1971).

Ruprecht, T. K. and Wahren, C.: *Population programmes and economic and social development* (Paris, OECD Development Centre, 1970).

Sternberg, M. J.: "Agrarian reform and employment: potential and problems", in *International Labour Review* (Geneva, ILO), Vol. 103, No. 5, May 1971.

Symonds, R., and Carder, M.: *The United Nations and the population question* (London, Chatto & Windus for Sussex University Press, 1972).

Tabah, L.: *Rapport sur les relations entre la fécondité et la condition sociale et économique de la famille en Europe,* paper submitted to the Council of Europe Second European Population Conference, Strasbourg, 1971.

United Nations: *A concise summary of the world population situation in 1970* (New York, 1971; Sales No.: E.71.XIII.2).

— *Final Act of the International Conference on Human Rights, Teheran, 22 April to 13 May 1968* (New York, 1968; Sales No.: E.68.XIV.2).

— *Human fertility and national development: a challenge to science and technology* (New York, 1971; Sales No.: E.71.II.A.12).

— *Measures, policies and programmes affecting fertility, with particular reference to national family planning programmes* (New York, 1972; Sales No.: E.72.XIII.2).

— *The determinants and consequences of population trends* (New York, 1953; Sales No.: 1953.XIII.3) (Revised edition in preparation).

The American Assembly: *The population dilemma*, edited by Philip M. Hauser (Englewood Cliffs, NJ, Prentice-Hall, 1963).

World Bank: *Population planning*, Sector working paper (Washington, DC, 1972).

Wynn, M.: *Family policy: a study of the economic costs of bearing children and their social and political consequences* (Harmondsworth, Penguin Books, 1972).

VI. NOTES ON THE PHOTOGRAPHS

Facing p. 6—(*a*) During the early years of the nineteenth century, in Europe, overcrowding and bad sanitation resulted in epidemics of typhus, smallpox and cholera which carried away many thousands of children. However, public health and housing legislation, coupled with advances in medical knowledge, brought about a considerable improvement in health and living standards, with the result that by the second half of the century it became possible to rear most of the children successfully, and families with five children and more became common. This photograph of a middle-class Swiss family was taken about 1880. (*Photo:* Bibliothèque publique et universitaire, Geneva)
(*b*) These sturdy infants attending a nursery school in western Africa are the children of industrial workers living in a model town of 30,000 inhabitants planned and constructed by a public corporation. It is expected that in 20 years time the town will accommodate 400,000 persons—a remarkable example of controlled urban development. The vast majority of Africa's swelling population, however, have little chance of sharing such opportunities. (*Photo:* WHO/Paul Almasy)

Facing p. 7—The other side of the picture, and, sadly, the more common one. This child growing up in a riverside slum on the outskirts of a rapidly growing metropolis in the Far East is an Asian, but he could just as well be from any developing country with a high rate of population growth. Millions of people live in worse conditions, in shanty towns with no permanent structures. (*Photo:* © CIRIC, Geneva)

Facing p. 22—(*a*) Many rural workers in the Third World live in huts without ventilation or sanitation. Such conditions are not necessarily a direct result of excessive population growth. General poverty and lack of the technical knowledge to build better dwellings are undoubtedly major factors. But rapid population growth makes bad worse; sharpens poverty; increases overcrowding. (*Photo:* ILO)
(*b*) A large family and a new house. On the high plateau of the Andes the descendants of the Incas of Peru, for long amongst the world's forgotten peoples, are gradually carving out a better life for themselves, with inter-

national assistance. When the ILO's Andean Programme was launched in 1954, houses with windows were unknown on the plateau. (*Photo:* ILO)

Facing p. 23—An aged silversmith crouches over his bench. The proportion of old people is relatively low in the Third World because of the huge child population, but the absolute numbers are increasing as the expectancy of life improves. Little can be done for them, since the demands of a younger generation drain the greater part of a nation's resources. Many sociologists have argued, nevertheless, that the comparatively low cost of providing pensions would ease the labour market in countries with mass unemployment. (*Photo:* ILO/Paul Almasy)

Facing p. 70—Many hands, they say, make light work. In fact, the work is heavy enough on this construction site in India. In countries where capital is scarce and labour plentiful, it is often sound economics to employ men rather than machines. It also gives purpose to lives that might otherwise be wasted. When the dam is finished, it will bring life-giving water to land that was formerly barren: the earth, too, can be underemployed. (*Photo:* © CIRIC, Geneva)

Facing p. 71—(*a*) These men are building a nation—and a dam. Stone by stone, the huge structure takes shape, a monument as well as an investment. Every piece is inched to the site by human labour. To Western eyes, the workers bowed under their load seem to belong to another age; but if this policy were abandoned there would be no employment, no dam, and no future for the densely populated land. (*Photo:* David Channer. © Camera Press Ltd, London/Len Sirman Press, Geneva)
(*b*) The two worlds of urban man. In the foreground, parts of the ever-spreading shanty town on the outskirts of the metropolis. Beyond, the modern city. The influx from the countryside into the main cities of most developing countries is so rapid that the authorities can seldom provide the newcomers with water, sanitation, lighting or other municipal services. (*Photo:* © CIRIC, Geneva)

Facing p. 86—In a country where children are plentiful, parents poor and a good education difficult to obtain, child labour is not easy to eliminate. This youngster, moreover, is luckier than many of his generation, who beg in the streets or live by petty theft. He is, after all, serving some sort of apprenticeship. (*Photo:* R. Bersier. © CIRIC, Geneva)

Facing p. 87—(*a*) The paradox of child labour in a world where millions of able-bodied men have no work still affronts the nations' conscience. These small porters with their heavy loads are quite possibly the children of unemployed parents, or at any rate of parents who do not earn enough by themselves to feed and keep their family. (*Photo:* © CIRIC, Geneva)
(*b*) An unemployed worker from a developing country arrives in Europe, to try his luck in a strange land. Labour migration is not always from a densely populated to a thinly populated area. Often, indeed, the reverse is the case. It is rather the high rate at which the labour force—and the demand for

unskilled labour—is growing that keeps the human tide flowing. (*Photo:* ILO/Jean Mohr)

Facing p. 118—The sign means "Garden school", and the small boys with man-size tools are cultivating vegetables which will become part of the school meal. At the same time, they are acquiring basic farm skills and learning the value of a balanced diet. This is an example from Latin America of the more realistic approach to education now found in many developing countries. (*Photo:* © Len Sirman Press, Geneva)

Facing p. 119—(*a*) Learning to plough in a land where until recently the hoe was the only tool known in rural areas for breaking the soil. To arrest migration to the towns, and at the same time to feed the swelling population in both town and country, many developing countries have embarked on simple but effective schemes of rural development. This photograph was taken on a village training farm in western Africa. (*Photo:* ILO/Maya Bracher)
(*b*) Ideally, husband and wife should jointly decide on the number of their children. In this family planning clinic in eastern Africa the women are encouraged to bring their husbands. The trained nurse is explaining the reproductive process and the use of simple contraceptives. Such centres may be assisted by the World Health Organization and other United Nations agencies if the government so desires. (*Photo:* WHO/E. Schwarb)

Facing p. 134.—In several developing countries with official family planning programmes, social workers respected by the community are used to spread the notion of family planning. In this photograph a public health visitor is using a picture of a happy child to drive home her point. (*Photo:* WHO/Paul Almasy)

Facing p. 135—The four faces pictured behind the modern-style rickshaw's seat represent India's concept of a model family. The slogan reads: "Limiting your family to two or three children will make for a happy home." To spread the notion of family planning, the Indian authorities keep up a quiet, persistent campaign which pervades the nation's life. The aim is a generation which accepts family planning as a matter of course. (*Photo:* ILO/E. Schwarb)